3.95

*Tests
and Measurements*

LEONA E. TYLER

Professor of Psychology, University of Oregon; Diplomate in Counseling Psychology; author of books in the fields of individual differences, developmental psychology, and counseling, as well as numerous journal articles; researcher in the measurement of interests and the evaluation of choices.

Tests
and Measurements

PRENTICE-HALL, INC., *Englewood Cliffs, New Jersey, 1963*

TESTS AND MEASUREMENTS, *Leona E. Tyler*

PRENTICE-HALL FOUNDATIONS
OF MODERN PSYCHOLOGY SERIES
Richard S. Lazarus, *Editor*

Designed by Harry Rinehart

Foundations
of Modern Psychology
Series

The tremendous growth and vitality of psychology and its increasing fusion with the social and biological sciences demand a new approach to teaching at the introductory level. The basic course, geared as it usually is to a single text that tries to skim everything—that sacrifices depth for superficial breadth—is no longer adequate. Psychology has become too diverse for any one man, or a few men, to write about with complete authority. The alternative, a book that ignores many essential areas in order to present more comprehensively and effectively a particular aspect or view of psychology, is also insufficient. For in this solution, many key areas are simply not communicated to the student at all.

The Foundations of Modern Psychology is a new and different approach to the introductory course. The instructor is offered a series of short volumes, each a self-contained book on the special issues, methods, and content of a basic topic by a noted authority who is actively contributing to that particular field. And taken together, the volumes cover the full scope of psychological thought, research, and application.

The result is a series that offers the advantage of tremendous flexibility and scope. The teacher can choose the subjects he wants to emphasize and present them in the order he desires. And without necessarily sacrificing breadth, he can provide the student with a much fuller treatment of individual areas at the introductory level than is normally possible. If he does not have time to include all the volumes in his course, he can recommend the omitted ones as outside reading, thus covering the full range of psychological topics.

Psychologists are becoming increasingly aware of the importance of reaching the introductory student with high-quality, well-written, and stimulating material, material that highlights the continuing and exciting search for new knowledge. The Foundations of Modern Psychology Series is our attempt to place in the hands of instructors the best textbook tools for this purpose.

Preface

An elementary statistics teacher is often reminded of the popular record album "Classical Music for People Who Hate Classical Music." This book has grown from my attempts to teach the basic principles of psychological measurement to people who do not consider these principles to be of *central* importance in their life and work. We usually find, for example, that first-year psychology students do not wish to be mathematical statisticians. They realize, however, that the courses in psychology they intend to take require some knowledge of quantitative research methods and test techniques. Similarly, most teachers and counselors do not see themselves as test experts, but they know that it is important for them to be able to interpret correctly the information about individual students they get from standardized tests. With the enormous increase in the use of psychological tests in many areas of American life, more and more persons need the same kind of limited but basic knowledge—parents, businessmen, and readers of popular magazines, to mention just a few.

In my attempt to meet this need, I have found it useful to distinguish between *producer* and *consumer* knowledge. I have deliberately omitted or de-emphasized many concepts and methods that are essential in carrying out research or constructing standardized tests. And I have deliberately stressed the concepts one needs in order to read a journal article, choose a test to serve a particular purpose, or interpret an individual's score. Needless to say, such a distinction cannot be made sharply, and perhaps no two psychologists would make it in precisely the same way.

My primary aim has been to make the basic ideas *clear*. I am aware that this purpose has led to what some readers may consider to be oversimplification of definitions and computational examples. But I am assuming that a student who really comprehends the underlying themes will be able to assimilate the many variations without too much difficulty. Obviously, this little book is not intended as a substitute for thorough courses in statistics and psychological testing. On the contrary, it is my hope that it will encourage many students to continue their exploration of this extensive and fascinating terrain.

Leona E. Tyler

Contents

Contents

Contents

xi

*Tests
and Measurements*

The Nature
and Function
of Measurement
in Psychology

One of the principal distinctions between present-day
scientific psychology and the philosophical psychology of
times past or the everyday psychology of the man in the
street is an emphasis on quantity as well as quality, on
numbers as well as words. To the beginning student in
psychology this fact often comes as an unwelcome sur-
prise. Examining such unfamiliar quantities as means,
averages, standard deviations, and frequency distributions; weighing probabilities; making difficult decisions
among uncertain conclusions—these kinds of mental activity do not fit in with his preconceptions about

3

1

psychology or with his hopes about what he may learn from it. He may feel that in having to come to grips with them he is being asked to make a long detour over a rough and dusty road instead of proceeding directly to his goal— a working knowledge of human nature.

But the fact is that quantitative thinking is an essential rather than a peripheral feature of psychology today. The progress made during the last century would, indeed, have been impossible without it. In the first place, quantitative methods permit us to draw precise conclusions from experiments. In conducting an experiment, what we do is to apply some special procedure to animal or human subjects, and note its effects. But it is apparent to any careful observer that reactions to stimulating situations *vary* a great deal from person to person. At a sudden clap of thunder, for instance, one person rushes to the window to catch sight of the lightning flashes, another buries her face in her hands. So, too, in experiments, reactions vary greatly. Without some way of answering the questions "How much?" and "How many?" the outcomes of almost all experiments involving more than one subject thus become contradictory and confused. And unless we study more than one subject, we cannot expect to find out much about human nature.

In studying the learning process, for example, a psychologist may wish to find out whether it is better to present assignments in elementary logic so that students are prevented from making errors or so that they are permitted to make errors and then correct them. (Such questions become important when we undertake the practical task of constructing programs for the so-called "teaching machines.") In setting up an experiment to answer this question, the psychologist would work out ways of quantifying the performance of his subjects in as many aspects as possible. Anticipating that they will not all react in the same way to the experimental conditions, he will not be surprised if some persons score higher under Condition A, some score higher under Condition B, and some do equally well under both. And it may turn out that Method A enables some subjects to learn very rapidly, but at the cost of not retaining what they learn, whereas Method B may take longer but facilitate retention. Clearly, the psychologist must have many complex possibilities in mind as he plans the experiment.

So he would resort to different kinds of measurements to enable him to evaluate these possibilities. Thus, he might measure first the time each subject requires to reach a certain level of performance. He might give a test of logical thinking immediately after the experimental procedure, and again a month later. He might devise tests for other kinds of mental ability thought to be related to logical reasoning, such as practical problem-solving or the detection of errors in propaganda. For each set of scores, he would compare the averages for Groups A and B, making use of statistical methods that would permit him to come to a conclusion stated in terms of probabilities.

What he reports, then, would take this form: "In my sample Method B came out better, and there are less than five chances in a hundred that a difference of this size could have arisen in a sample from a population in which no true difference existed." Without quantifying his data he could have drawn no conclusions at all; with quantification he can make a statement of *probability* upon which to base further decisions—either to proceed with one of the methods or to do another experiment.

Thus measurements help psychologists make decisions about what their research means. They also facilitate decisions about individuals. Psychologists began their efforts to construct mental tests because tools that would help make such decisions were needed. The ancestor of our present-day intelligence tests was Alfred Binet's 1905 scale. Binet developed this test as a means for helping Parisian school authorities decide which children were really unable to profit by the regular school program, no matter how they tried. Whatever can be said about the misuses of intelligence tests from Binet's time to our own—and there are many serious and valid criticisms that can be made—they have in countless instances enabled teachers to distinguish between the dull and the lazy far more efficiently than they could otherwise have done.

Let's take another example. During World War II, all branches of the Armed Forces would probably have preferred to recruit men who were above average in intelligence and emotional stability, high in mechanical and clerical aptitudes, athletically skilled, and physically fit. Obviously, though, there are very few such all-round men. The problem for military psychologists, then, was first to find out what *particular* abilities and skills were needed in particular military jobs. Next, they devised tests to measure these abilities, and finally they assigned men to special programs on the basis of their scores. If, for example, the work of a personnel clerk requires mainly quick perception of details in written material, a knack that clerical aptitude tests measure, the sensible procedure seemed to be to assign to the personnel program men who rated high on clerical tests but not so high on mechanical tests. The men who scored higher on mechanical than clerical tests would be left for assignment to other training programs, such as that for airplane mechanics. Because there were many more or less distinct aptitudes or specialized mental abilities to be measured and millions of recruits to be assigned, the decision-making task the military psychologists faced was extremely complex. They did not always succeed in assigning individuals where they could make their most effective contribution, but the number of satisfactory placements was far higher than it would have been had they relied on verbal descriptions rather than numerical scores. Quantification was an indispensable tool in the assignment of individuals to training programs.

Another kind of decision about persons has fostered a whole family of tests and measurement techniques. As more and more people have become interested in mental health and aware that psychological ills can be treated, demand for *personality tests* has grown. When a patient comes to a mental hospital or clinic, it is helpful to determine at the outset what kind of person he is and how he is likely to respond to treatment. Take the case of, say, Lawrence Gibbs. Should his condition be labeled "schizophrenia" or "anxiety reaction"? His psychiatrist may be looking for clues about whether Gibbs will respond better to hospital treatment or to therapy at a clinic in his own community. And if he enters the hospital, should he be assigned to a therapy group, or would some form of individual treatment carry a better prognosis? These are complex decisions that can seldom be made with any great certainty, but personality tests of several kinds can help in making them.

Measurement techniques are important also in situations where individuals must make decisions about their own lives. In some ways, these decisions *by* a person are more complex than decisions *about* a person. Many of the factors entering into them cannot usually be quantified—highly personal factors such as Henry's knowledge that his mother will be terribly disappointed if he does not go into the ministry, or Mr. Merton's feeling about a job that requires him to be away from home for long periods of time. But the fact that there are quantitative answers to some questions often simplifies such situations enough so that satisfactory decisions can be reached. The score on one kind of test, for example, will tell a college senior who is trying to decide whether to go on to graduate school or to go into business how he compares in complex intellectual abilities with successful graduate students in his major area. The score on another kind of test will enable him to judge how similar his interests are to those of both businessmen and scholars in his field. Day after day, in high school and college counseling offices, psychological measurements contribute to such decisions.

Thus, testing techniques and the statistical methods that go with them have been woven into the whole fabric of general and applied psychology. We shall now examine in more detail the ideas and the tools that are used. Real skill in the use of these methods requires a long apprenticeship, but a general understanding of the basic principles is within the reach of everyone who applies the findings of modern psychology to himself and to those around him—in short, anyone, as parent, teacher, businessman, or just plain citizen.

LEVELS OF MEASUREMENT

Measurement, as psychologists use the term, covers a wide range of activities. The only thing they all have in common is the use of numbers. The most general definition of measurement we can formulate is simply that measurement means the assignment of numerals according to rules.)

These *rules* are not always as restrictive as persons with limited mathematical knowledge often think they are. Unless we have given the matter a good deal of thought, we are likely to assume that all the operations of elementary arithmetic—addition, subtraction, multiplication, and division—ought to be applicable to all measuring systems. Thus, our first reaction may be to conclude that measurement is impossible unless some arithmetical operation can obviously be applied. Take the whole field of intelligence testing, for example. Ever since these tests first came into use, thoughtful persons have pointed out that it really makes no sense to say that a boy with an IQ of 150 is twice as bright as a boy with an IQ of 75. That the boys are very different in their response to situations calling for abstract reasoning is true, but there is no justification to be found anywhere in their behavior for expressing this difference as a quotient of two, a fraction of one-half, or a ratio of two to one. It is just not meaningful to *divide* one IQ by another.

Once psychologists became aware of this peculiarity in some of the numbers they were using, they realized that there were parallel situations outside psychology. Take temperature, for example, as we ordinarily measure it on our Fahrenheit or Centigrade scales. If the temperature drops from 80° F during the day to 40° F during the night, we do not say that it was half as warm at midnight as it was at noon. Because zero in the Fahrenheit system is an arbitrary figure that does not really mean "no warmth at all," the number of degrees above zero cannot be handled in the same way that a measurement of height or weight can. Clearly, measurements of intelligence are more like those of temperature than those of height.

The general formulation of different kinds, or levels, of measurement that has been most useful to psychologists is the one set up by S. S. Stevens.* According to this system, we can divide the possible ways of assigning numerals into four types. Each of these varieties of measurement has rules and restrictions of its own. And, for each, certain statistical procedures are appropriate.

The Stevens system, as shown in Figure 1 on page 8, arranges these levels of measurement according to the extent familiar arithmetical procedures are applicable. The first, or lowest, in the series is the *nominal* scale. Where this kind of scale applies, numbers are assigned only to identify the *categories* to which individual persons or things belong. These can be one-of-a-kind classifications, like placing numbers on football jerseys to identify the players. Or they can be labels that apply to *groups* of persons, as when men are given

*See the chapter "Mathematics, measurement, and psychophysics" in his *Handbook of experimental psychology* (New York: Wiley, 1951).

LEVEL	LIMITATIONS	ILLUSTRATION
IV — RATIO SCALES Each number can be thought of as a distance measured from zero.	There are no limitations. All arithmetical operations and all statistical techniques are permissible.	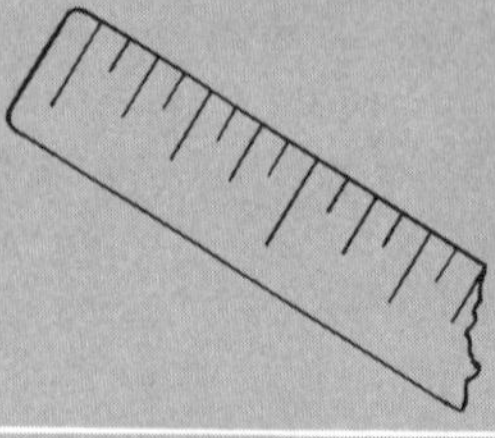
III — INTERVAL SCALES The intervals or distances between each number and the next are equal, but it is not known how far any of them is from zero.	In addition to procedures listed below, addition and subtraction and statistical techniques based on these arithmetical operations are permissible. Multiplication and division are not permissible.	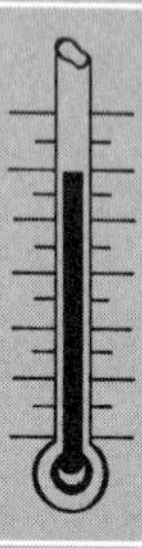
II — ORDINAL SCALES Numbers indicate rank or order.	In addition to procedures below, ranking methods and other statistical techniques based on interpretations of "greater than" or "less than" are permissible.	
I — NOMINAL SCALES Numbers are used to name, identify, or classify.	The only permissible arithmetical procedures are counting and the statistical techniques based on counting.	

Figure 1. The levels of measurement.

a code number of 1, women a code number of 2. The only arithmetical operation applicable to nominal scales is counting, the mere enumeration of individuals in each class. The identifying numerals themselves can never be added, subtracted, multiplied, or divided.

The next level of measurement is the *ordinal* scale. We use this when we are able to arrange individuals in a series ranging from lowest to highest according to the characteristic we wish to measure, but cannot say exactly how much difference there is between any two of them. When a committee ranks five scholarship candidates for over-all merit, they are using an ordinal scale.

The percentile scores often used in reporting test results to students, since they too are a kind of ranking, also constitute ordinal measurement. The common arithmetical operations—addition, subtraction, multiplication, and division—cannot be legitimately used with ordinal scales, but statistical procedures based on ranks are appropriate. It is possible, for example, to determine whether the ranks of a group of children on popularity are related to their ranks on dependability.

The third level of measurement is the *interval* scale. What distinguishes interval from ordinal measurement is that it permits us to state just how far apart two things or persons are. Most school tests are of this type. Although there is some question about their measurement properties, teachers usually regard the scores on course examinations as interval scales. They consider it legitimate to compare the scores two students make and to tell Jerry that his score is 16 points lower than Bill's. But interval scales do have one important limitation. They have no real zero point. It is true that a student may occasionally come out with a *score* of zero on a test of trigonometry or English literature. But this does not mean that he has no knowledge whatever of the subject. Although the purpose of the test is to measure knowledge of subject matter, it is not really necessary to define what "zero knowledge" means in order to do so, since we will be using the test mainly to compare individuals with one another.

Though we may add and subtract scores on interval scales, one arithmetical operation is never legitimate—that is, to *divide* one score by another, since division presupposes the existence of an exact zero point. Why not? Consider for a moment an examination in which Louise scores 80 and Marie 40. Now suppose that in writing this examination, the instructor had happened to include 10 other questions easy enough for both girls to answer correctly. In this case Louise would have scored 90, Marie 50. The difference between their scores would be 40 points in either case, but the quotient of the two scores would not be the same. Instead of 2 (80 ÷ 40), it would be 1.8 (90 ÷ 50). With any particular test, then, we have no way of finding out whether one person's knowledge is twice as great, three times as great, or one-and-a-half times as great as that of another person. But if we can assume that each question is an equally good indicator of knowledge of the field, we do not violate any principles of mathematics or logic when we subtract one score from another or when we add a number of scores together and take an average. The statistical methods used to translate raw scores on tests into various kinds of derived scores—methods we shall be considering in a later chapter (see pp. 35–38)—rest on addition and subtraction exclusively.

The fourth and highest level of measurement is the *ratio scale*. With it all arithmetical operations can be used—addition, subtraction, multiplication, and division. Ratio scales have all the charactertistics of interval scales, with the additional advantage of a true zero point. We are probably more familiar with such scales than with any of the other types because all common physical dimensions—height, weight, volume—can be measured this way. On the scales of an honest butcher, zero means that no meat at all has been placed on the pan, and when we buy from him we can confidently say that a six-pound roast is four pounds heavier than a two-pound roast; it also makes sense to say that it is *three times* as heavy. The name *ratio scale* signifies that we can divide one number by another or express the two as a ratio.

Many of the measurements we make in psychology fail to qualify as ratio scales, but a few of them do. These few usually occur where it is possible to measure a mental characteristic in physical units of some sort. When we measure reaction time, for example, we use the customary time units, seconds and fractions of a second. If we are interested in determining how quickly would-be automobile drivers can step on a brake pedal in response to a red light, we can do so with a ratio scale. Thus, if it takes John five-tenths of a second and Bill only three-tenths of a second, we can, if we like, make a 3:5 ratio of these two scores to describe how much quicker Bill is than John. Still, even when we are working with a ratio scale, as in this instance, we may not wish to make ratios or divide one number by another. For all the methods permissible at lower levels of measurement can be used at a higher one. In practical applications of studies of reaction time, for instance, what the investigator would probably want to know about both John and Bill is how they compare with norms, or standards, for adequate drivers. Such comparisons involve only subtraction, not ratio-making.

Most of the scales psychologists have worked with are of the ordinal and interval varieties. *If we recognize this and observe the limitations that go with such measurements, we reach sound conclusions; if we do not, many kinds of errors creep into our reasoning.* Without some knowledge of the kinds of tests and measurements that have been used in psychology, the importance of this statement may be hard to grasp, but an illustration may help to clarify it. As we have said, percentile scores on tests constitute ordinal scales. This limits the use of these scores in that we must consider only the order in which they are arranged; we must not assume that the intervals between successive scores are equal. What does this mean practically? Let's consider two high school seniors who are discussing with a counselor their scores on a test of college aptitude. As always on the percentile scale, the average score for the group being considered is 50. Now, Sheldon has a score of 60, which means that 60 per cent of a norm group of college applicants score lower than he does. Jeff has a score of 40, which means that 40 per cent of the group of college applicants score below him. Clearly, 60 is above average, and 40 is below. But in order to help the boys reach correct conclusions about these "unequal unit" ordinal scores, the counselor must be aware that the units on the percentile scale are *large* for very low or very high scores, but *small* for those near the average. Because of this fact, scores of 60 and 40 are both very close to 50. Any conclusion that Sheldon should go to college but that Jeff should not would be completely unwarranted. Both boys have an *average* chance of college success. What this means for practical purposes is that persons without any knowledge of basic statistics must be very cautious in drawing conclusions about the meaning of differences expressed in percentiles. If one knows something about ordinal scales he will at least be aware of the necessity for caution.

With this fundamental understanding that numbers do not always mean what we think they mean, let us turn to some of the statistical ideas we must grasp if we are to use psychological measurements intelligently.

Basic Statistics

At the beginning of the previous chapter, we raised the problem of variation from person to person. More than a century ago, Lambert A. Quetelet, a Belgian mathematician, discovered a kind of order in individual variations that impressed him deeply. Quetelet worked mainly with census data and measures of physical characteristics, but it was not long before Sir Francis Galton, the brilliant English scientist, was applying Quetelet's methods, and others he himself developed, to measurement of characteristics like "acuteness of vision"—traits we would now classify as psychological.

12

2

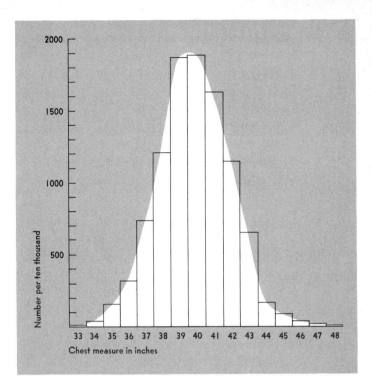

Figure 2. Chest measurements of 5738 soldiers. (From Galton, F. Hereditary genius: an inquiry into its laws. Appleton, 1870. Horizon Press, 1952, chapter 3.)

The method these early workers hit upon—one that has been in constant use ever since—was to obtain measurements on a large group of individuals, and then arrange the results in order from lowest to highest in what they called a frequency distribution. In these distributions they found the same pattern showing up again and again, a pattern that can be illustrated by Galton's measurements of the chest girths of more than 5000 soldiers, shown in Figure 2.

The pattern, when a distribution is pictured in a graph, is a bell-shaped curve. A large number of cases clusters near the middle of the distribution, forming the average, or central tendency. The farther from this average a measurement lies, the smaller the proportion of the total group to whom it applies. Thus, there are many men with chest measurements of 39, 40, and 41 inches, but only a few with as low as 33 or as high as 48. Quetelet, Galton, and other nineteenth-century workers found such a beautiful regularity in the distributions of trait after trait that they came to believe there was some universal law governing human differences.

This symmetrical, bell-shaped curve was already familiar to mathematicians. They had discovered it as they studied the outcomes of games of chance —coin-tossing, dice-throwing, and the like—and had worked out the mathematical equation for the curve of the distribution obtained with an infinitely large number of events, each determined by what we call "chance." This *normal probability* curve (or *Gaussian* curve, as it is called in honor of the mathematician who formulated its equation) became one of the foundations of modern statistics. To Quetelet and Galton, the equation for it seemed to apply equally well to the distributions of measurements they had collected. The word "normal," as used in statistics, applies to this curve and carries no connotation of "right" or "best."

As time has passed, it has become clear that human measurements, especially measurements of psychological traits, do not always yield a Gaussian distribution. Some distributions are *skewed,* meaning that there are either too many high scores or too many low scores in the group to produce the symmetry of the normal distribution curve; others are too *peaked* or *stretched out* to fit the normal curve equation. These require special equations. But since statistical methods based on normal distributions are easier to use and interpret than those based on less common mathematical formulations, testmakers often make a special effort to collect items that will result in a normal distribution in the group for which a test is intended. Thus, if the group on which preliminary norms are based turns out to have too many low scores, it is possible to take out some of the harder test questions and replace them with

Figure 3.   Distribution of IQ's on form L of the Stanford-Binet test for ages 2½ to 18. (From McNemar, Q. The revision of the Stanford-Binet Scale. Boston: Houghton Mifflin, 1942.)

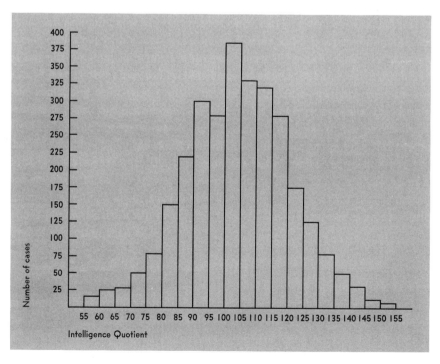

easier ones. If there is not enough spread, items can be added that will produce more low and high scores. For some testing purposes, non-normal distributions are deliberately sought. In short, methods for analyzing the characteristics of each question in a test now make it possible to select items in a manner that will produce any desired distribution. The majority of well-standardized tests yields normal distributions when large groups are tested.

In Figure 3 we see such a distribution for a test that was for years the leading measure of children's intelligence. While there are a few minor irregularities, they are not great enough to constitute a serious departure from the normal form. There are large numbers of IQ's in the neighborhood of 100, very few near the extremes of 55 and 155. (A very small proportion of the population scores lower and higher than the arbitrary end points shown here.)

MEASURES OF CENTRAL TENDENCY

In summarizing a distribution of measurements for a group, we must always report two characteristics. First, we must describe in some way the *central tendency,* most commonly by computing what we ordinarily call an average, but what statisticians call the *arithmetic mean.* To get this figure, we simply add all the scores together and divide by the number of cases. There are two other kinds of averages, however, that are preferable for some distributions—the median and the mode. The. *median* is simply the *middle* score in a distribution, or the number that would represent a point between the two middle ones. The *mode* is the *most common* score, the one made by the most persons. In Table 1 on page 16, we see what the mean, median, and mode would be for one set of figures. We can also see why we might prefer one to the others. A parent who wished to pay his child for allowance an amount that conformed to the central tendency of the group might well be dissatisfied with the arithmetic mean as an average here. This is why: The two boys in the group who receive $1.00 allowances are not at all typical. Adding these figures in with the others inflates the total so that the mean, 29¢, is too high to be really characteristic of the group as a whole. The median of 22½¢ seems fairer in this case. But the most convenient index of central tendency here is the mode of 25¢, the amount received by the greatest number of boys.

In a distribution that is exactly normal, the mean, median, and mode are identical, so it makes no difference which one we use as a measure of central tendency. Since few distributions turn out to be *exactly* normal, however, we must usually decide which is the most convenient and meaningful. Often the choice depends on what other uses we plan to make of the scores besides just citing an average.

TABLE 1

Central Tendency Determinations for a Distribution
of Weekly Allowances Received by 20 Boys in a School Class

Boy	Allowance	Boy	Allowance
1	$.10	11	$ .25
2	.10	12	.25
3	.10	13	.25
4	.15	14	.25
5	.15	15	.25
6	.15	16	.30
7	.20	17	.30
8	.20	18	.35
9	.20	19	1.00
10	.20	20	1.00

Mean   = $5.75 ÷ 20 + $0.2875, or $0.29
Median = Between $0.20 and $0.25, or $0.23
Mode   = $0.25

MEASURES OF VARIABILITY

The second kind of index we need in order to describe a distribution of scores is some measure of *variability*. How much of a *spread* is there in the distribution? It obviously makes a difference to a schoolteacher, for example, whether the range of reading scores in her class is from 50 to 150 or from 90 to 110. In both classes, the average score is about 100, but the first group would require much more diversification of reading materials than the second one would. The simplest way to describe this variability is to subtract the lowest score from the highest one. This gives us the index called the *range*. In the example just given, the range in the first classroom is 100 points, in the second 20 points.

The disadvantage of the range is that a single high or low score tends to carry too much weight. In a group of 1000 school children, for example, there may be only one who receives a score of 100 on an arithmetic test. The next highest person scores 82. To say that scores range from zero to 100 is a little misleading and gives the wrong impression about how variable the *group* actually is. A far more satisfactory index of variability in a group, one that does not unduly emphasize extreme cases, is the *standard deviation*. The formula is $SD = \sqrt{\dfrac{\Sigma d^2}{N}}$ (where d stands for "deviation from the mean," N, of course, stands for the number of persons in the group, and the Greek symbol Σ stands for "sum," thus instructing the reader to *add* the numbers to which it applies, in this case all squared deviations). Table 2 shows how it is computed. First we obtain the mean, or average, score in the customary way. Then we subtract this figure from each of the individual scores. Next we

TABLE 2

Computation of the Standard Deviation
for a Distribution of the Scores
Made by 11 Children on a Spelling Test

Child	Score	Deviation from Mean	Squared Deviations
Elaine	20	+6	36
Martha	18	+4	16
Bill	15	+1	1
Jim	15	+1	1
Edna	14	0	0
Harry	14	0	0
Marie	14	0	0
Joe	13	−1	1
Lucy	13	−1	1
John	10	−4	16
Grant	8	−6	36
	154		108

Mean $= 154 \div 11 = 14$
Variance $= 108 \div 11 = 9.82$
Standard deviation $= \sqrt{9.82} = 3.1$

square each of these deviations. To find out what the *average* of these squared deviations is, we divide their total by the number of cases, which gives us what statisticians call the *variance* of the distribution. To obtain the *standard deviation* we take the square root of the variance.

It is readily apparent that the standard deviation does not have the defect we noted in the range—its magnitude does not depend greatly on single extreme scores. On the contrary, each score in the distribution contributes to the standard deviation. In distributions where scores cluster quite closely around the mean, the standard deviation will naturally be small. In distributions where scores spread out a good deal on both sides of the mean, the standard deviation will be large.

Where the distribution of scores is normal, a person who knows the mean and standard deviation does not need to *see* the whole distribution in order to grasp its major characteristics. The use of means and standard deviations thus furnishes us with a valuable shorthand way of comparing groups and individuals within groups. We will explain in more detail in a later section how we make such comparisons.

MEASURES OF RELATIONSHIP

Besides measures of central tendency and variability, one other statisticial device is indispensable in dealing with measurements of human traits. When, as is often the case, we must *relate* one score to another, we use the *correlation coefficient*. Although there are many ways of computing correlations, one technique, which yields an index called the *product-moment coefficient*, is the most common.

It is also possible—and helpful—to indicate graphically, by a scatter diagram, the extent to which two measures are related. So, before we delve into the computation of the product-moment coefficient, let us look first at Figure 4, a scatter diagram that plots the correlation between the spelling scores of the 11 children in Table 2 and their arithmetic scores. On the graph one mark indicates each child's scores in both subjects. Martha's scores, for example, are on the line extending upward from a spelling score of 18 and on the line extending to the right from an arithmetic score of 25. In a diagram

Figure 4. Scatter diagram showing relationship between spelling and arithmetic scores made by 11 children.

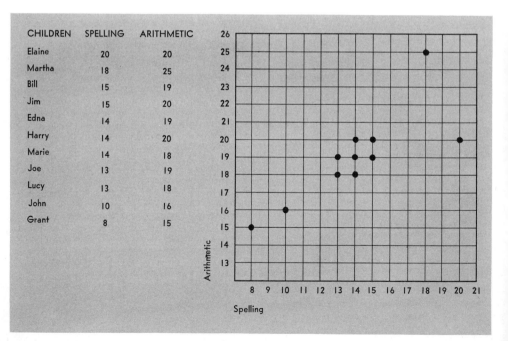

CHILDREN	SPELLING	ARITHMETIC
Elaine	20	20
Martha	18	25
Bill	15	19
Jim	15	20
Edna	14	19
Harry	14	20
Marie	14	18
Joe	13	19
Lucy	13	18
John	10	16
Grant	8	15

of this sort, we can judge how closely related two measurements are by seeing how closely the entries lie to a single line that might be drawn from the lower left to the upper right corner. If all entries are on such a line, the relationship between the two scores portrayed is perfect. In this case, it would mean that each child was exactly as much above or below the group average in arithmetic as he was in spelling. This is not quite the case, however, for the scores in Figure 4. There is a strong general trend for scores to fall *near* such a diagonal line, but they are not exactly *on* it. A scatter diagram gives a vivid but rough picture of such a relationship. We often need to refine our understanding.

The product-moment correlation coefficient (r) is a precise mathematical statement of the relationship between two such sets of scores. Its formula is:

$$r = \frac{(dx)(dy)}{N(SD_x)(SD_y)}$$

(In this formula the letter d, again, stands for deviation from the mean, N stands for the number of cases, SD_x stands for the standard deviation of the first set of scores, and SD_y stands for the standard deviation of the second set of scores.) Table 3 on page 20 shows how we compute it. First we find the mean and standard deviation for each set of scores. (These are computed for spelling scores in Table 2; the same procedure is followed for the arithmetic scores.) We then multiply each person's deviation from the group mean for spelling by his deviation from the group mean for arithmetic. The algebraic sum of these deviation *products* forms the numerator of the fraction in the equation. We then proceed to obtain the denominator in the fraction by multiplying the number of cases by the product of the two standard deviations.

If the relationship between two variables is perfect, r will be 1.00. For all lesser degrees of relationship, it will turn out to be a decimal number less than 1.00. In our example, $r = .83$. We can understand why this is as high as it is, and also why it is not 1.00, if we examine the deviations. The children who are above average on the spelling test are also above average on the arithmetic test, except for Bill. The children who are below average in spelling are also below average in arithmetic, except for Joe. Elaine is a little higher in spelling than Martha is, while Martha is higher than Elaine in arithmetic. But generally speaking, each of these children is just about as successful in arithmetic as he is in spelling. It is precisely such correlations that a high correlation (here .83) indicates. Just as the mean and standard deviation are shorthand descriptions of one distribution, so a correlation coefficient provides a summary of the relationship between two.

Many of the correlations the psychologist runs into are lower than the one we have been considering, and sometimes they are negative. A negative

TABLE 3

Computation of the Product-Moment
Correlation Coefficient for Scores
Made by 11 Children on Spelling and Arithmetic Tests

Child	Spelling	Arithmetic	Spelling Deviation from Mean	Arithmetic Deviation from Mean	Product of Deviations
Elaine	20	20	+6	+1	+6
Martha	18	25	+4	+6	+24
Bill	15	19	+1	0	0
Jim	15	20	+1	+1	+1
Edna	14	19	0	0	0
Harry	14	20	0	+1	0
Marie	14	18	0	−1	0
Joe	13	19	−1	0	0
Lucy	13	18	−1	−1	+1
John	10	16	−4	−3	+12
Grant	8	15	−6	−4	+24
					+68

Spelling mean $= 154 \div 11 = 14$
Arithmetic mean $= 209 \div 11 = 19$
Spelling standard deviation
   (computed in Table 2) $= 3.1$
Arithmetic standard deviation
   (computed in manner shown in Table 2) $= 2.4$

$$\text{Product-moment correlation } (r) = \frac{68}{(11) \times (3.1) \times (2.4)}$$
$$r = .83$$

correlation in our example would have told us that low scores in spelling tend to go with high scores in arithmetic, and vice versa. Had the correlation turned out to be about zero, it would have told us that there is *no* relationship, in other words, that the whole range of combinations of low and high scores in arithmetic and spelling occur equally often. A moderate correlation, such as .50, would reveal that individuals tend to score about as high in one trait as they do on the other but that there are numerous exceptions to this general trend.

Correlation techniques have been indispensable in the development of usable mental tests. Had we not been able to analyze what characteristics are *related* to one another, we should never have been able to find out what a new test measures or how accurately it measures anything at all. Just how correlations are used for these purposes will be considered in the next chapter, which is on tests.

So far we have been looking at statistical methods designed to *describe* distributions compactly. But statistics also provides convenient techniques for making *inferences* about *other* persons and events that are not part of a group originally studied. The methods used for this purpose are sometimes complex and difficult to understand, but anyone who works with psychological measurements should have the basic reasoning behind them within his grasp.

The fundamental idea is that any one group of persons or things we choose to measure constitutes a *sample* of a larger population. When we carry on research, it is that general population about which we really wish to draw conclusions rather than the particular sample we happen to test. Thus, the 11 children whose spelling and arithmetic scores we have been examining are only a small part of a numerous group of children their age. Whether the population of ten-year-olds we are interested in is in one town, one state, one country, or the whole world, the principle is the same: These children constitute a sample; we would like to infer from their scores something about spelling and arithmetic performance in the population.

The problem of how samples are related to populations has been studied through both practical procedures and mathematical reasoning. In the practical, empirical kind of study, an investigator may shake dice again and again, work out the mean of each ten throws, and analyze the differences among these "chance" samples of ten from a "population" that consists of, say, 10,000 throws. Mathematical reasoning accomplishes the same purpose with less effort. What we find in both cases is that the drawing of repeated samples from the same population produces a *distribution* of whatever statistic we are computing—a normal one if the population from which the samples were drawn has a normal distribution. The mean and standard deviation of this *sampling distribution* can be estimated from the information we have about a few samples, or even one sample alone. In Figure 5 on page 22 we see what the sampling distribution of means for samples of 25 would be for a population with a mean of 100 and a standard deviation of 20. We need not go into the mathematical relationships or the formulas used to make the computations. The only important point to be gleaned from Figure 5 is that the variability of the *means* of samples of 25 is *much smaller* than the variability of scores in the population from which samples are drawn.

There is a special name for the standard deviation of the *sampling distribution,* a standard deviation that indicates how much variability there is in

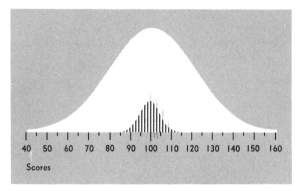

Figure 5. Hypothetical normal distribution of scores for an infinitely large population in which the mean is 100 and the standard deviation is 20. Also the hypothetical distribution of means that would be obtained if many samples of 25 were drawn at random from such a population.

a *statistic* rather than in people or events. It is *standard error*. Since we can compute any statistic we like in samples and in populations, there are many kinds of standard error—standard error of a mean, standard error of a difference between two means, standard error of a correlation coefficient, standard error of a score. For whichever kind, the standard error is a way of showing us what degree of variation, with regard to the statistical unit in question, we can expect in different samples of the same population.

The concept of sampling distributions enables us to determine the probability that any result we have obtained could have occurred by "chance." Chance is simply a label for whatever unknown factors there are that cause samples to differ. Why does one throw of the dice turn up different numbers from another? Chance. Why do answers on a public opinion poll vary a little from group to group, even when respondents are chosen in exactly the same way? Chance.

To illustrate this reasoning, let us compare some scores to find out whether the difference between two means is a matter of chance. Suppose that the teacher of our 11 children adopts a new method whereby she hopes to make them better spellers. After a month of intensive training under the new method, the children take a second test known to be exactly equal in difficulty to the first one. Their scores on the first and second tests are shown in Table 4. It is clear that the average for the class had gone up from 14 to 16. While there was one child who actually scored lower on the second test than he did on the first, the rest all improved to varying extents. But is this 2-point difference really large enough so that we *know* that it could not have occurred by chance if we had taken a second sample of these children's spelling without giving them any special teaching at all? It is this sort of question that the *t* statistic was designed to answer. What *t* is, is the ratio of the difference between means to the standard error of the difference. (There is, of course, one other possibility—that the 2-point difference represents not chance variation but a gain resulting from what was learned by taking the first test. To allow for this would require a more complicated research design. For the time being, we will ignore the possibility.) Before considering what t means, let us see how it is computed.

First of all, we determine the difference between the two scores for each individual in the group. Then we work out the mean and standard deviation of this distribution of *differences* just as we do for single scores. (In one respect this computation differs from the one shown in Table 2. In inferential, unlike descriptive, statistics, for reasons it is not necessary to go into here, we divide the total of the squared deviations by one less than the total number of individuals in the group, in this case by 10 rather than 11.)

TABLE 4

Computation of the *t* Statistic
to Test Whether an Increase in Spelling Scores
Is Statistically Significant

Child	First Score	Second Score	Difference	Deviation from Mean of Difference	Squared Deviation
Elaine	20	23	+3	+1	+1
Martha	18	20	+2	0	0
Bill	15	19	+4	+2	+4
Jim	15	15	0	0	0
Edna	14	11	−3	−5	+25
Harry	14	16	+2	0	0
Marie	14	18	+4	+2	+4
Joe	13	15	+2	0	0
Lucy	13	16	+3	+1	+1
John	10	13	+3	+1	+1
Grant	8	10	+2	0	0
	154	176	22		36

Mean of first test $= 154 \div 11 = 14$
Mean of second test $= 176 \div 11 = 16$
Mean of differences $= 22 \div 11 = 2$
Standard deviation of differences $= \sqrt{36/10} = \sqrt{3.6} = 1.9$
Standard error of difference $= \frac{1}{9} \div \sqrt{11}$

$$= \frac{1}{9} \div 3.3 = .6$$

$t = \dfrac{2 \text{ (Difference mean)}}{.6 \text{ (Standard error of difference)}}$
$\quad = 3.3$
$P < .01$

To get the standard error of the difference between two means (the standard deviation of the sampling distribution for such differences), we divide the standard deviation of the differences by the square root of the total number of cases. (Again, we need not go into the mathematical reasons for this procedure.) The t ratio consists of the mean of the differences divided by the standard error of the differences. In this case, it turns out to be 3.3. From tables of t, available in all standard statistics texts, we learn that this is statistically significant at the .01 level (represented as $P < .01$ in Table 4).

This last phrase, translated into the language of samples and populations and applied to our example, means that no more than once in a hundred times would a group of children like ours give us the results we obtained on the two tests if chance factors alone were operating. We can conclude with some confidence, then, that the special teaching method *was* effective. It might not, of course, be effective for the reasons the teacher thinks it is. Other try-outs of the method under various conditions, as well as comparisons with groups taught in other ways, would probably be necessary before the teacher could be sure just why it worked.

There are many other versions of the t formula designed to be used with different kinds of data. But whatever technique is used, the outcome is a probability statement like the one in the example. These probability statements are what the term *statistical significance* refers to. A statistically significant difference is one that produces a t with a *small* probability. This means that it is *not* very likely that the difference in question would occur in chance samples in which the members had not been chosen in a special way or given special treatment. A statistically significant correlation is one that would have been unlikely to turn up, had we simply put down pairs of numbers at random and gone through the motions of computing r. The lower the probability value, then, the more certain we can be that our results represent something other than chance.

Anyone who reads research reports will repeatedly encounter such phrases as "significant at the .05 level." This is simply a way of stating what we have been talking about—of saying that results like those reported would have been expected by chance not more than five times out of a hundred. It is customary not to consider results that give probabilities larger than .05 to be "statistically significant," but the level varies somewhat in accordance with what the investigator is trying to find out.

The development of statistical techniques that permit research workers to make inferences about whole populations from samples has enabled us to increase our knowledge far more rapidly than we could otherwise have done. Besides that, however, an understanding of these techniques, at least in a general way, is useful to any intelligent citizen who is not himself a research worker, in that it helps him to evaluate what he hears and reads about people and products, to draw some conclusion as to whether figures presented as evidence for the superiority of a new tooth paste, for example, really prove anything. Intricate as the reasoning included in statistical inferences is, it is well worth the effort to master it.

Psychological Tests

TESTS VERSUS MEASUREMENTS

So far we have not considered whether there is any distinction between the terms *test* and *measurement*. Although their meanings overlap, they are not quite synonyms. The latter word applies in many areas of psychological research where the former would not be appropriate. For example: Experimenters who study sensation, perception, and judgment make extensive use of *psychophysics*, that is, the measurement of physical magnitudes corresponding to psychological magnitudes (such things as how bright a light looks, or how loud a tone sounds). If the question under examination is, say, "What

25

3

are the upper and lower limits of human hearing?" what they measure are vibration rates. The physical measurements are thus used to answer a psychological question.

A measurement is called a test only if it is used primarily to find out something about an *individual* rather than to answer a general question. Measurements of pitch thresholds can, of course, be used as tests. But more typically a test consists of questions or tasks presented to the subject, and the scores obtained are not expressed in physical units of any kind.

Thus, not all measurements are tests. But the reverse is also true—not all tests are measurements. There are some personality tests, for example, that do not produce scores. A psychologist may use such a test to help him formulate a verbal description of a person. Measurement, at any of the levels we distinguish in Chapter 1, need not be involved. In Chapter 1 *measurement* was defined as the assignment of numerals to things according to rules. A *test* can be defined as a standardized situation designed to elicit a sample of an individual's behavior. When that sample can be expressed as a numerical score, either test or measurement is an appropriate term.

Thus, even though the overlap between the concepts is not complete, we can still say that most tests are measuring techniques, and most psychological measurements can be used as tests. We shall take up in this chapter some ideas that apply particularly to tests.

HISTORICAL BACKGROUND

Throughout the years since psychology got started as a scientific enterprise (the date usually cited is the establishment of Wilhelm Wundt's laboratory in Leipzig in 1879), researchers have focused their efforts primarily on the search for general principles that would apply to everyone. Psychologists have tried to discover how the human eye and brain work together to produce the perceptions of color, shape, and size we all experience. They have set up experiments to study the learning process, expressing their findings as "laws of learning." They have studied human development, by comparing one age group with another, and have established norms of behavior for each age.

All along, however, there has been a secondary focus of interest and effort. Even some of the earliest workers in the then-new German laboratories of experimental psychology turned their attention to the *variation* they encountered among subjects. These men were often persons with a strongly practical orientation who realized that measurements of differences among people might have important applications in schools, factories, and offices.

An American who studied in Wundt's laboratory, James McKeen Cattell, was particularly influential in the movement to utilize psychological measurements as mental tests. It was he, in fact, who first used the term "mental test," in 1890, but there were others who figured prominently in the same movement during the closing years of the nineteenth century.

What these scientists were most eager to find was some quantitative way of assessing general intelligence. They thought they could obtain an index of intelligence if they could measure in combination in individuals all the characteristics that were being measured separately in the experimental laboratories—sensation, perception, attention, discrimination, speed of reaction, and so on. The superior man, according to their reasoning, should be the person who ranks high in all these qualities. Though there is nothing obviously wrong with their reasoning, the attempt to measure intelligence in this way failed. For when the psychologists analyzed their measurements, they discovered that these traits were not closely correlated one to another. Furthermore, the sum of the scores did not appear to be an index of general intelligence. Poor students, for example, achieved just as high scores as good students did. Clearly, a different approach to the problem of measuring intelligence seemed to be required.

This new departure was soon made in France, when Alfred Binet started from the premise that intelligence is an inherently *complex* characteristic, not merely the sum of many simple traits. To measure it, he held, we must find ways of evaluating how individuals deal with tasks that require reasoning, judgment, and problem-solving. So over a period of years Binet tried out —on his own children and on children of different ages in the Paris schools— many kinds of tasks as potential tests of children's intelligence. At last in 1905, with the collaboration of Thomas Simon, he published the first real intelligence scale, the ancestor of all our present tests.

Progress was rapid from then on. The Binet-Simon scale was adapted for use in many countries. Tests suitable for adults were added to those designed especially for children. Group tests were produced during World War I and adapted soon afterward for use in schools and industries. Tests for many abilities not so broad and general as intelligence were constructed. Attempts to measure personality characteristics as well as abilities became more and more common. By the middle of the 20th century, thousands of tests—good, bad, and indifferent—were in print.

In the course of all this activity on the mental testing front, standards and principles emerged. These now serve as convenient guides to those who wish to construct new tests and to those who need to select wisely from the ones already available. Furthermore, in our test-conscious modern world, it has virtually become essential for an educated man or woman to know something about these standards and principles. The teacher who wishes to adapt class-room instruction to the differing characteristics of the children in her charge, the parent who wants to help his son or daughter make wise plans for educa-tion and career, the businessman who hopes to avoid being duped by un-scrupulous test publishers and salesmen—all need a working knowledge of how tests are built and how they should be judged.

THE MEANING OF VALIDITY

The most important consideration is *validity*, which pertains to the ques-tion: *"What* does this test measure?" Unless we have a fairly adequate answer to this question, any test will be useless in our attempts to deal wisely with human beings—adults or children, ourselves or others. It may even be worse than useless, because if we act on the wrong assumption about what a person's score means, we may steer him toward decisions that will lead to maladjust-ment and costly mistakes.

Many persons fail to recognize that the title of a test really tells us nothing at all about what the test measures. Anyone can write a set of questions, and he may be perfectly confident that they call for "reasoning" or "mechanical aptitude" or "cognitive flexibility" on the part of the respondent. But to find out what mental processes the testee must actually use to answer these ques-tions is a long and arduous task. A test Mr. Smith constructs to measure "reasoning ability" may prove to be a test of middle-class attitudes. A "mechanical-aptitude" test may turn out to measure mainly general intelli-gence. An "emotional-maturity" inventory may measure only what testees know about the social desirability of certain behavior. The first knack one must acquire in evaluating the validity of tests is the habit of disregarding their titles. The important question is not "What does the author *call* this test?" but "What are scores on this test *related to?*"

At the outset of the testing movement, the accepted procedure was to define first what one *intended* to measure and then collect evidence to show how successful one had been. During those years, as we saw, most efforts were directed toward the measurement of general intelligence. And although it be-came apparent as the number of investigators increased that they were not all defining this elusive term in exactly the same way, still, for practical purposes they were all assuming that intelligence is the trait on which judgments of brightness and dullness in school are based. Thus they looked to school situa-tions for evidence about the validity of intelligence tests. How close, they asked, is the relationship between the degree of school success predicted from test scores and the degree of success actually achieved? It was on the basis of the resulting evidence that the laboratory measurements of discrimination, reaction time, and the like, were discarded, and the Binet-type questions, calling for more complex responses, were retained in intelligence tests.

Such measurements of a psychological trait in a real-life situation such as a schoolroom are called *criterion* measurements. Correlations between test scores and criterion measurements are called *validity coefficients*.

To start with, then, validity meant *the extent to which a test measures what it purports to measure*. To find out how valid a test was, one was expected to correlate test scores with criterion measurements. But as time passed, it became clear that there were complications in both procedure and concept. Unfortunately, it is impossible in most instances to find any one criterion that will be an unambiguous indicator of a mental trait. Two psychologists investigating the same trait—mechanical aptitude, for example—may decide to use different criteria and so may achieve different results. Mr. Allen may think that the obvious measures to rely on are the grades high school boys receive in a shop course. Mr. Baker may think that the length of time it takes new men to learn a simple mechanical skill in a factory is the relevant criterion. Now, what if the test they both use correlates .06 with one of these criteria, .59 with the other? How are we to say how valid the test is when it gives results of this sort? Is it a test of mechanical aptitude or not?

Out of experiences like these the realization has grown that the validation of a test is a long *process* rather than a single event. Only through studying the test's correlation with a variety of criteria can we understand just what it is measuring. A series of research studies on the "mechanical-aptitude" test, for example, may demonstrate that what it really measures is the ability to carry out finely controlled, skilled movements and that it has nothing to do with the ability to grasp complex relationships of mechanical parts. Thus, it may correlate fairly highly with grades in wood shop but not with grades in machine shop. It may select competent workers for one factory but not for another.

Therefore, instead of asking the old validity question, "To what extent does this test measure what it purports to measure?" we are now more likely to ask, "Just what is it that this test does measure?" Today, we know that we must analyze the content of the test and examine many correlations with different criteria in various groups before we can know the answer. And as we do, our knowledge of what the basic mental *traits* are and how they relate to one another continues to grow and change along with our knowledge of the individual tests themselves. It is not really necessary that a psychologist formulate at the beginning a precise definition of the trait he hopes his test will measure. If he has a general idea about the characteristic and its relationship to either theoretical concepts or practical situations, his precision in defining it will increase as he tries out his test in a series of separate research studies.

Understanding what is involved in the validation of tests carries three clear implications for test-users. One is that if a test is to be employed in making decisions about individuals or groups, all the available evidence should be studied before any attempt is made to interpret the scores. This means that someone in the organization using the test must be capable of making such a study. A "testing program" in schools or in industry can function effectively only when it is run by a thoroughly competent person.

Another implication is that whenever possible a test to be used for prediction or selection (as of job applicants) should be validated in the specific situation in which it is to be employed. This, of course, requires a special research study on the spot before one begins to use the test routinely to decide which applicants to hire. The relevant validity question to ask when such a study is planned is not "Is the test valid?" but "Will this test add anything to the validity of selection methods now being used?" A college that has been applying definite standards of selection on the basis of high school grades may find that a so-called "college aptitude" test has nothing to contribute to its program. Another college, with a different program, which draws from a different pool of applicants, may find that the same college aptitude test has considerable validity. Not all situations permit this on-the-spot validation of tests, however. But where it is possible, it is to be highly recommended. For an example of a study of the predictive validity of the Iowa Tests of Educational Development, made especially for high school teachers, see Table 5. It shows, for instance, that tenth-graders who score 25 or 26 are likely to succeed in college. Out of every 100 students with scores this high, 91 make at least a 2.0 (C) average, 70 make a 2.5 (C+) average, and 40 make a 3.0 (B) average.

Finally, whether we wish to use tests in practical situations involving individuals or in pure research aimed at increasing our theoretical knowledge of individual differences, we should always remember that our ideas about what the *traits are* as well as what the tests measure must change as new evidence comes in. When a research worker fails to get the correlation he expected between "anxiety" and "susceptibility to the stress of failure," he may need to change his views about what is being measured by the anxiety scale he has been using. In addition, he may have to modify his theory about the way personality is affected by the threat of failure. Persons who use special tests a great deal, such as teachers in the public schools, should try to keep abreast of new knowledge about these tests and also about the qualities they measure. Many present-day school teachers, for example, are making decisions about children on the basis of outmoded *concepts* of what intelligence is. What they need is not just more valid tests but a more penetrating

TABLE 5

Some Evidence about the Validity
of the Iowa Tests of Educational Development
as Measures of Ability to Do College Work

ITED Composite Score (test taken in 10th grade)	*Chances in 100 of Earning College GPA of*			F	*Expected Range of College Grades*			
	2.0	2.5	3.0		D	C	B	A
29–30	97	86	62					
27–28	95	80	50					
25–26	91	70	40					
23–24	86	60	29					
21–22	78	49	19					
19–20	60	38	13					
17–18	59	28	8					
15–16	48	19	4					
13–14	38	12	2					
11–12	27	7	1					
9–10	18	4						
7–8	12	2						
5–6	7	1						
3–4	4							
1–2	2							

Most Probable Grade

(For ITED Forms X-1, X-2, Y-1, Y-2)
$N = 365$ $r = .55$

For Students at University of Oregon
and Oregon State College.

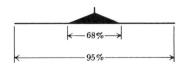

|←— 68% —→|

|←———— 95% ————→|

of Actual Grades Fall Within These Ranges

From Carlson, J. S., and Fullmer, D. W., *College Norms* (Eugene, Oregon: University of Oregon Counseling Center, 1959), p. 11.

knowledge of what the word intelligence means. We cannot really explore test validity without examining at the same time the validity of our own ideas.

Validity is the most important consideration in the construction and use of all types of test. Next in order of importance is *reliability*. In explaining what this is, we can start again with a question: How accurately or how consistently does a test measure whatever it does measure?

When a person takes a test, many things may influence his score, quite apart from the ability or personality trait the test has been designed to measure. If the testee is distracted or rebellious, he may not give as many good answers to questions as he would if he were concentrating on the task. This produces a score that is lower than it should be. On the other hand it may happen that he has encountered the night before, on a television program or in casual conversation, some of the specific questions contained in the test. In this case he is likely to obtain a score that is a little higher than his customary performance would entitle him to. These are two examples of *chance* influences on test scores. There are innumerable others—emotional reactions to the examiner, temperature and ventilation in the examining room, good or bad luck in making guesses about things one really does not know, to mention just a few. They are all essentially unpredictable, and they do not affect all testees in the same way or to the same degree.

What the test-maker must discover and communicate to the test-user is how inaccurate individual scores are likely to be because of such chance factors. Having this information, the person who must interpret a score can make the proper allowance for such inaccuracy. His conclusion about a person will then follow these lines: Billy is slightly above average in intelligence. There is a 50-50 chance that his IQ lies somewhere between 105 and 115. He will not conclude: Billy has an IQ of 110.

There are a number of ways to analyze the reliability of a test and report the results of the analysis, but they all have the first step in common: the administration of two versions of the *same* test to a group of persons typical in age or social characteristics of the people for whom the test is intended. If we want to determine the reliability for eight-year-olds of a particular test of intelligence, we may give a group of eight-year-olds both Form A and Form B simultaneously. If only one form is available, we can construct separate scoring keys for two halves of the test—usually the odd items on one key, the even items on another—so that we obtain two scores for each person rather than one. If we want to evaluate the reliability of a test of finger dexterity for boys at a vocational school, our procedure will probably be to administer the test to a group of boys twice, with a short interval between sessions. This procedure also gives the examiner two scores for each subject. In each example, there is no reason to suppose that all the miscellaneous chance determiners influence both scores the same way. Therefore, we can reason that the more *alike* the two scores for each person are, the more consistently, or accurately, or *reliably,* the test is measuring some nonchance ability or personality trait. But the more cases there are in a group of individuals who make very different scores, the more we can suspect that the scores of all testees depend to a large extent on chance factors.

As we saw in Chapter 2, the standard way of stating the degree of resemblance (or difference) between two sets of scores is the correlation coefficient. Because chance influences are always present to some extent, a test-maker never finds *perfect* consistency between two sets of scores; the correlation, that is, never turns out to be 1.00. But if the test is well constructed and is administered carefully under good conditions, it is not too much to expect that this *reliability coefficient* should be about .90. For some purposes and in some situations, a test can still be used even though its reliability is considerably lower than this. What is important is that the person who makes inferences about individuals or groups on the basis of the test should *know* how reliable it is so that he can make the necessary allowances for inaccuracies.

Unfortunately, describing the reliability of a test by citing the correlation between two versions of it has several disadvantages. The most serious is that a correlation turns out to be higher if there is a great deal of range, or spread, in the scores of the group on which it is based than it does if the members of the group score closer together. Thus, the user, in evaluating the reliability of a test for a certain purpose, should insure that the reliability coefficient is based on a group with about the same amount of diversity as the one he is working with. The Army General Classification Test, for example, is reliable enough to distinguish levels of general mental ability in army recruits, representing as they do an extremely wide variety of natural gifts and educational attainments. But it is not reliable enough to distinguish with any clarity between one college student and another. A psychologist who expected to use this test in a university counseling program would be misled if he judged its reliability by a coefficient based on data obtained from a group of run-of-the-mill recruits. What he needs to look at is a reliability coefficient based on information pertaining to a group of college students.

Fortunately, there is another way of reporting how accurate or inaccurate scores on a test are, the *standard error of measurement*. We have explained the general meaning of the term *standard error* in Chapter 2. This particular version of that statistic gives an estimate of the range of variation in a person's score if he were to take the same test over and over again an infinite number of times—if, in other words, we could draw many "samples" of the test scores in his whole "population" of scores. This range is a zone of inaccuracy on either side of an obtained score. The logical and statistical foundations on which this method rests are too complex to be set forth here, but the final interpretation is relatively simple to grasp.

If the standard error of measurement for an intelligence test, for example, is 4.6, there is a probability of about two-thirds that an individual's true score is within 4.6 points of the score he has actually obtained. If Greg gets a score of 154, we can conclude with some assurance that his "true score," free from chance influences, probably lies somewhere between 149.4 and 158.6. This follows from the fact that in any normal distribution, about two-thirds of the cases fall within one standard deviation of the mean. As explained previously, the standard error is a special kind of standard deviation. There is still one chance in three that his "true score" is higher or lower than this, and we can if we wish, using reasoning based on the concept of standard error, say that there is a 5 per cent probability that it might even be as low as 145 or as high as 163. (This is because, in a normal distribution, about 95 per cent of the cases fall within two standard deviations of the mean). But ordinarily we do not try to make such exact determinations. We use the standard error as a guide to the general amount of inaccuracy we should allow for in interpreting scores and making decisions about individuals. If the intelligence test in the foregoing example is used to select students for an honors program, and the decision has been made that all students who score 155 or higher are eligible, Greg with his score of 154 does not at first glance seem to qualify. But a teacher who takes unreliability into consideration will recognize that Greg may belong in the select group, for the probability is fairly high that his true score is at least 155. In such a case the teacher would look very carefully at various supplementary evidence to find out what kind of student Greg is before deciding whether or not to assign him to the special class. Understanding what reliability means can thus make a real difference in the use of tests in making decisions. (In stressing the fact that tests are not altogether reliable we must always remember that other ways of evaluating people are unreliable too. A test-maker tells us how much inaccuracy to allow for. Usually we have no way of knowing how much we should allow for in teachers' judgments, for example.)

A person who does not understand what test "reliability" means may let his general evaluation of a test be influenced too strongly by statements about its reliability. For the word "reliable," as used in our common speech, carries *favorable* connotations—a reliable ("good") man, a reliable ("upstanding") firm, a reliable ("worthwhile") product. Teachers, personnel workers, and clinicians are all too likely to conclude that a reliable test is, *ipso facto,* a *good* test for any purpose they have in mind. Such errors can lead to serious misjudgments of people. Evidence that a test is accurately measuring *something* tells us very little. We need to know much more about the test. Until we know *what* the something it measures is, we are not justified in drawing conclusions about people from the scores they make. As we saw in the previous section, the task of finding out just what a test does measure is long and arduous. "Reliable" does not mean "good" for everything. Validity remains more important than reliability.

In evaluating tests and interpreting their scores, we must consider, in addition to reliability and validity, the various units in which those scores are expressed. A score that indicates only how many questions a person answered correctly does not tell us very much about the person unless we have some standard of comparison. If Leonard brings home a report that his score on a school arithmetic test was 47, the first question his mother is likely to ask is, "What kind of scores did the other children get?" The derived, or transformed, scores used with standardized tests of aptitudes, achievement, and personality are designed to facilitate just such comparison of individual scores with group norms. We can go about the job of deriving, or transforming, scores in several ways.

The simplest way of accomplishing this is to set up *percentile* norms for a group and transform each person's score into an equivalent percentile rank. To construct tables of percentile norms, simply divide by the total number of persons in the group the number of those who rank below each raw score *plus* one-half of those who receive exactly the score in question. If, in the intelligence test example on page 34, 91 out of a class of 100 high school sophomores score below 154, Greg's score of 154 gives him a percentile rank of 91 in this group.

The other common method of translating scores into equivalents that indicate where an individual stands in a group makes use of the mean and standard deviation as a basis for norms. In normal distributions there is a fixed relationship between the distance from the mean and the area under the curve; Figure 6 on page 36 shows what this relationship is. Regardless of how large or small the standard deviation is in any particular group of scores, it can be used as a meaningful unit of distance along the base line. In a normal

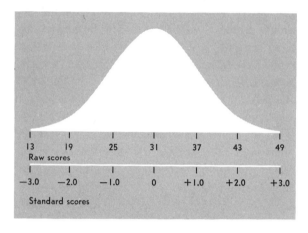

Figure 6. The standard scores corresponding to raw scores at different levels for a distribution in which the mean is 31 and the standard deviation 6.

distribution, if we measure off one standard-deviation unit from the mean, we find ourselves directly under the point where the curve changes from convex to concave. Three such units measured off from the mean, and we reach a point very near the end of the distribution. Thus, if we wish, we can state in standard-deviation units how far each score is from the mean and indicate in this way where each one fits into the total distribution. Instead of reporting a score as 25 for someone in the group represented in Figure 6, we can report it as —1.0 standard-deviation unit (or —1σ, in the Greek-letter notation often used). As soon as he sees the latter, anyone familiar with the normal distribution curve knows just about how far below average the subject is.

This kind of transformation has enabled psychologists to make comparisons that would not be possible with the raw scores themselves. In another normal distribution of test scores (see Figure 7), the mean may be 178 and

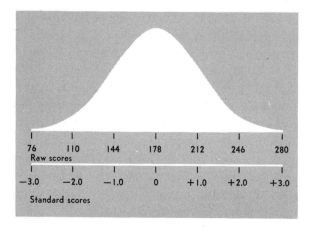

Figure 7. The standard scores corresponding to raw scores at different levels for a distribution in which the mean is 178 and the standard deviation 34.

the standard deviation 34. The numbers along the base line for raw scores are different from those shown in Figure 6, but the standard scores are the same. A score of 144 on this second test (178 minus 34) is just as low as a score of 25 on the first one. Both are reported as −1.0 standard deviation (or −1σ).

For convenience, we often express basic standard scores in many other ways. In order to provide measurements divided into finer units, for instance, we can multiply all numbers by 10 so that they range from −30 to +30 instead of from −3 to +3. Then, in order to eliminate negative scores, we can add 50, so that they range from 20 to 80, with 50 instead of zero as the mean. Neither of these transformations, though, changes in any way the fundamental relationships between scores. In Figure 8, we see how a number of these derived scores as well as the percentile scale are related to the basic normal distribution. Values in vertical alignment on the various horizontal

Figure 8. Relationships between various types of derived scores. (Seashore, H. G. Methods of expressing test scores. Psychological Corporation Test Service Bulletin, *No. 48, 1955.)*

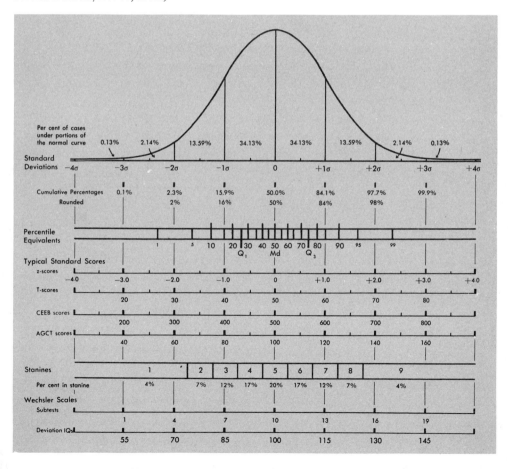

lines beneath the normal curve will be equivalent if the norm groups on which they are based are similar.

In addition to percentile ranks and standard scores, there are various other ways of making scores meaningful. We will consider the IQ in the next chapter. Age and grade norms for school achievement tests require no special explanation.

In order to organize the whole complex and confusing field of psychological testing, we must somehow classify tests and isolate the common characteristics of each group rather than concentrate on the special qualities of particular tests. There are many possible ways to do this. For one, we might use as a basis for classification the form of the test, that is, the way questions are presented. The principal distinction here is between individual and group tests. An individual test is, in effect, an interview in which the examiner asks questions and writes down the testee's answers. A group test is set up so that instructions can be given to many testees at the same time, each of them writing his own answers. Another distinction, which often cuts across this one, is between paper-and-pencil and performance tests. In the first the testee thinks about the problems presented and writes down the results. In the second he manipulates the test materials themselves, such as toys, picture cards, or blocks.

A third basis for classifying tests is content. The principal distinction here is between language and nonlanguage tests (or verbal and nonverbal tests). Note that this is not identical with the previous distinction. Paper-and-pencil tests can fall in either the language or nonlanguage category, and so can performance tests. Written nonlanguage tests often use pictures rather than words or numbers; even the directions can be given in pantomime. Within each of these main content categories, further distinctions based on content are possible—verbal versus numerical or pictorial versus geometrical, for example.

Still another distinction that may be of considerable importance in some situations pertains to speed and power. In a speed test, a person's score depends on how many questions he is able to answer in the time allowed. In a power test, his score depends on the difficulty of the questions he can answer. Investigations have shown that many tests have both speed and power components, and that many, perhaps most, individuals, score at about the same level in both categories. But there are some situations and some individual cases where this is not true. For example, a rehabilitation counselor working with an arthritic patient may seriously underestimate his client's abilities if he gives him tests in which being able to write swiftly or move pieces around rapidly helps to determine the score. He needs tests in which crippled hands are not a handicap.

These criteria are all of enormous value, but perhaps the fundamental basis for classifying tests, and the one we shall use in this book, is what they are designed to measure. By this standard, we can distinguish three major classes of test, each with many subclasses. First of all, are the tests of general intelligence; second, the tests of special abilities; and third, the tests of personality qualities. Somewhere under these three headings most of the thousands of existing psychological tests find their places, and within each of the three groups we can discover the other distinctions we have outlined. Thus, of general intelligence tests, some are for individuals and some for groups; they vary greatly in type of content; and some are mainly speed tests, some mainly power tests. The distinctions in form and content are found in special-ability and personality tests as well; the category of power tests, however, is less applicable in the personality than the special-ability group.

We have considered in this chapter certain concepts and procedures that are applicable to all these varieties of test. But there are other concepts and procedures that apply to one of the three areas—intelligence, special abilities, and personality—more than to the others. We shall take these up in the chapters to follow.

Intelligence Tests

The attempt to measure human intelligence has entailed more continuous, long-term, intensive effort than any other project in psychological measurement. In the study of intelligence, philosophical curiosity interacts with practical demands. For centuries men have puzzled over the enormous differences in sheer intellectual capacity that separate a Socrates from an ordinary citizen, an idiot from a normal child. They have asked whether such differences are innate or acquired—whether biological or educational factors are more influential in producing them. Eventually, because of

4

the practical needs of civilized societies, it became more and more urgent to find some way to evaluate the intelligence of individuals as accurately as possible. The advent of universal education brought all sorts of children, talented and untalented, into the schools. Some appeared to be incapable of mastering the curriculum educators had planned for them. Others raced through it and busied themselves with scientific experiments and philosophical speculations long before they reached physical maturity. Clearly, teachers needed to be able to distinguish between different mental capacities in order to educate children suitably. Similar problems arose in military organizations and in industries in connection with attempts to fit individuals into appropriate positions.

When psychologists began their effort to measure intelligence, just before the beginning of the twentieth century, they lacked a precise idea of the nature of this quality. As we saw in the discussion of validity in the previous chapter, this situation is not unusual, nor is it necessarily detrimental. Even a vague idea about a human trait can serve to guide a testmaker as he selects test items and plans validity studies. Then, as evidence accumulates about what the test scores *are related to,* he is able to formulate increasingly clearer definitions of what the test measures and to modify and improve the test.

The first intelligence test for children, the Binet-Simon scale, had been preceded by a long period during which Binet had carefully observed differences in the thinking processes of children. From this work certain clues about what an intelligence test should be became apparent. First of all, he decided, it should reflect the rapid *growth* in mental capacity that occurs during childhood. Second, for practical reasons if for no other, it should tap the characteristics by which teachers differentiate between "bright" and "dull" children in their schoolrooms. Binet studied his own little daughters, talked to teachers about how they judged mental capacity, and carried out various experiments before he was ready to present an intelligence test to the public. His tentative definition of intelligence as measured by this first scale was "the tendency to take and maintain a definite direction; the capacity to make adaptations for the purpose of attaining a desired end; and the power of auto-criticism." As we have seen, the publication of an intelligence test at this particular time was stimulated by a request from the Paris school authorities for a method that would help differentiate between really dull children and others who were just lazy.

The idea caught on immediately. The Binet-Simon Scale itself went through two revisions, in 1908 and in 1911, and it was translated and adapted in many countries. In the United States Lewis M. Terman of Stanford University took up the idea and started working on an American revision. The result was the Stanford-Binet test, first published in 1916, revised in 1937, and brought up to date in 1960. For half a century the Stanford-Binet test constituted a virtually official standard for intelligence measurement, like the bars and weights in Washington that officially define for us our foot and pound. At present, however, more alternative tests are available than in previous years, and the tendency has diminished to refer all of intelligence measurement to the Stanford-Binet. But the part this test has played in the development of theoretical concepts and practical applications of mental testing can hardly be overemphasized.

DISTINGUISHING FEATURES OF BINET TESTS

It is not important to know how the successive revisions differed from one another or from the original Binet-Simon test. What is worth looking at is the body of features that characterize all versions. First, they are *scales.* This means that the constituent questions and tasks are grouped on the basis of their difficulty. Beginning with easy questions, the examiner asks harder and harder ones as the test proceeds. A child's score chiefly depends on how far *up* this ladder he can go, rather than on how fast or how fluent he is (though both speed and fluency are required in some of the individual tests). From Binet's 1908 revision on, the tests have been grouped by *age levels.* A great deal of effort has been expended on the task of finding out just what the age norms are. In order to assign a test to a particular age level, it is necessary to investigate how children of various ages handle it. The tests pegged at year ten, for example, must contain tasks that are in the scope of only a minority of nine-year-olds, a majority of ten-year-olds, and a much larger number of eleven-year-olds. Thus, an intelligence scale of the Binet type is built to measure *mental growth.*

The second shared feature of the Binet tests is that they yield a general *global* measure of intelligence rather than an analysis of separate special abilities. It is clear from Binet's definition that he thought of intelligence as a complex capacity for handling a great array of tasks rather than a sum of distinct abilities to do particular things. In keeping with this view, the tests for a single age level may require knowledge of words, perceptiveness in seeing details in pictures, reasoning, and immediate memory. No attempt is made to segregate types of ability. Figure 9, which shows the variety of materials used in administering the 1960 Stanford-Binet test, gives some idea of this diversity.

The third characteristic that distinguishes Binet-type tests from many others is that they are designed to be given *individually* by a skilled examiner (see Figure 10). It requires more skill than one might suppose to maintain a friendly, encouraging attitude toward the testee, while simultaneously

Figure 9. *Materials used in testing intelligence with the Stanford-Binet.* *(By permission, Houghton Mifflin.)*

Figure 10. *The administration of the Stanford-Binet test. (City College of New York Educational Clinic.)*

carrying out instructions to the letter. And these instructions are rigid. For example, the examiner must never change the wording of a question in any way—what might seem to him a minor modification may have the effect of making an item harder or easier than it was for the subjects on whom the age norms rest. The examiner may praise the testee in order to stimulate his best efforts, but he must not do so too often or at the wrong times. He may repeat some questions but not others. If it is not clear whether an answer meets the specifications for a given age level, he may ask a question, but he must be sure not to give the testee a clue to the right answer. To act natural, friendly, and relaxed while using procedures and words that are so rigidly specified requires a great deal of practice. Obviously, a Binet test cannot be given by just anyone who comes into possession of the materials.

Finally, the system of scoring in all Binet tests is tied to the age norms. A child's mental age, usually abbreviated MA, indicates the age group for which his performance would be typical. For example, an MA of 9-6 means that a child is as far along in his general mental development as the average nine-and-a-half year old. Thus, an MA is somewhat like the size of a boy's suit or a girl's dress. We tell people how big Susie is physically when we say that she wears a size 10. We tell them how "big" she is mentally when we say that her MA is 10.

THE MEANING OF THE IQ

The Stanford-Binet and other Binet-type tests also provide for the computation of an *intelligence quotient* (IQ). Until the 1960 revision, when statistical refinements were introduced, the IQ was figured simply by dividing the child's mental age by his chronological age, then multiplying the quotient by 100 to get rid of the decimal point. For example, a child whose MA is 10, but whose actual chronological age (CA) is 9 would have an IQ of 111 (10/9 $\times$ 100). The IQ indicates just *how* "big for his age" or "small for his age" a child is. It tells us something about his *rate* of mental growth up to the time we tested him.

Unfortunately, the term IQ became overly popular and was used in numerous unwarranted ways. Misconceptions about its meaning are, in fact, still common. It is *not* the all-important index of intellectual capacity it is often assumed to be. And it is *not* a measure of an *amount* of anything, but simply a way of indicating what a child's average growth rate has been. At one stage in the research on intelligence it was thought that growth rates would be stable enough throughout childhood to serve as a basis for accurate predictions of adult intelligence. But as more knowledge accumulated, it became apparent that the "constancy of the IQ" is far from absolute.

For one thing, even in tests that are standardized and allocated to age levels as carefully as they were in the 1937 revision of the Stanford-Binet scale, IQ's at different age levels are not entirely comparable statistically. A very bright child could obtain a higher IQ at twelve than he did at six, even if his growth rate had not changed at all, simply because the variability of the IQ distribution was greater for twelve-year-olds than for six-year-olds. For other published tests less carefully standardized, this variation in the meaning of high and low IQ's from age to age is even more troublesome.

For another inadequacy, the IQ is not an appropriate way to describe *adult* intelligence. Like physical growth, mental growth in adults lacks the predictable regularity it shows in children. From the mid-teens on, *age* standards are relatively meaningless. It makes no sense to say that 20-year-old Jim's mental age is 25, because 25-year-olds and 20-year-olds do not differ in their response to the material in intelligence tests. What looks like an IQ for an adult is really a standard score. It signifies that the person occupies the same position in the adult distribution as a child with that IQ would occupy in a similar distribution of children. As psychologists studied the complexities of IQ scores, they came to realize that *all* IQ's, for children as well as for adults, could be interpreted as standard scores. What an individual IQ really tells us is how many standard deviations above or below average a person is.

One of the most useful things a student can learn is not to pay too much attention to a numerical IQ. Many first-rate standardized tests now provide norm tables from which other derived scores may be obtained—scores that show directly where a person stands in a group with which he wishes to compare himself, such as, for example, seven-year-olds, high school graduates, or army recruits. The 1960 revision of the Stanford-Binet test, while it continues to employ IQ terminology, no longer provides for the computation of this score in the old way—that is, by dividing MA by CA. Instead, the examiner uses tables that show directly how different a child's score is from the mean, or average, of a representative group of children his own age. This derived score is *called* an IQ but is really a standard score. The IQ concept served us well in the early days of intelligence testing, but it is now being retired from active service.

THE WECHSLER TESTS

Besides Lewis M. Terman, who devised the original Stanford-Binet test, and Maud Merrill, who worked with him on the 1937 revision and prepared the 1960 revision, another American has been particularly important in intelligence measurement—David Wechsler. In 1939, Wechsler published a standardized set of individual intelligence tests designed especially for adults. It was called the Wechsler-Bellevue Scale (the second part of the name honored New York's Bellevue Hospital where Wechsler worked). This test immediately came into wide use because of the demand, with the unprecedented growth of clinical psychology during and after World War II, for the evaluation of intellectual ability in millions of adults. The Binet scale in its various revisions had met the needs of institutions serving children, but had never been entirely satisfactory with adults.

Since World War II, Wechsler has developed a scale for children built on the same plan as the original Wechsler-Bellevue Scale. He has also revised the adult scale thoroughly. The two current versions of Wechsler's tests, then, are the WAIS (Wechsler Adult Intelligence Scale), published in 1955, and the WISC (Wechsler Intelligence Scale for Children), published in 1949. Although the two overlap to some degree, the WAIS is principally designed for ages 16 and above, the WISC for ages 15 and below.

Wechsler includes many of the same kinds of questions and tasks that Binet, Terman, and others had used, but he combines them differently. Instead of grouping them by age levels, he assembles them by *type* of question or task, arranging the specific items within each set according to difficulty. For example, all the arithmetic questions are in one subtest, all the block-design tasks in another. The subtests in turn are grouped into two main classes labeled *Verbal* and *Performance*. The verbal tests included in the WAIS are headed Information, Comprehension, Digit Span, Similarities, Arithmetic, and Vocabulary. The performance tests are titled Picture Arrangement, Picture Completion, Block Design, Object Assembly, and Digit Symbol. The subtests in the WISC are similar with a few minor changes. Verbal tests include questions like these:

What is the population of the United States?
Why should we keep away from bad company?
How are an orange and a banana alike?
What do we mean by "fabric"?

Some of the performance tests are shown in Figure 11.

Wechsler has set up separate norms for each subtest. It is thus possible to see how an adult or child compares in each category with a group that is representative of the whole population. Further, we can add up the standard scores on the separate subtests to produce on over-all verbal score, an over-all performance score, and a total score. Finally, by comparing these three inclusive scores against norm tables for the subject's *age* we can read off his verbal, perform-

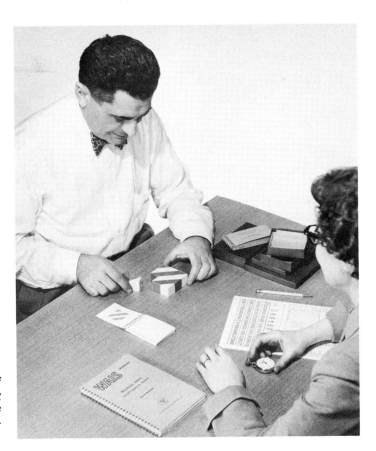

Figure 11. Samples of material used in testing intelligence with the WAIS. (The Psychological Corporation.)

ance, and total "IQ's." Such an IQ, however, like that obtained from the 1960 Terman-Merrill revision, is not an actual *quotient* of MA and CA. It is, instead, an indication in standard-deviation units of how the person relates to the average of his own age distribution. See Figure 8, page 37, for the relationship between Wechsler IQ's and the basic standard-deviation units in many other systems of derived scores.

It was hoped when these scales first became available that differences among scores on the separate subtests would facilitate diagnostic evaluations of mental functioning that would be helpful to clinicians and teachers interested in knowing more about an individual than on over-all score revealed. It seemed possible that an analysis of strengths and weaknesses shown on the various tests could help to answer such specific questions as: In which psychiatric classification does Mr. King belong? Has Mrs. Logan incurred some kind of brain damage? What particular educational deficiencies are handicapping Susan? As time has passed, though, statements about the diagnostic significance of score patterns, or profiles, have become more and more guarded. We know now that there are many possible reasons why Mr. Henderson may, for instance, score lower on *Arithmetic* than on the other tests. Such a discrepancy may indicate anxiety, but it may simply mean that the subject never really learned elementary arithmetic in the first place. Clinicians still analyze an individual's score profile and scrutinize his answers to specific questions, seeking for clues to help them understand him. But they have learned to regard the ideas generated this way as mere *hypotheses* to be checked against other information about the person.

Differences between verbal and performance scores are more meaningful than discrepancies between the scores on particular subtests. True, we must be cautious in interpreting these differences as well. Neither scale is so reliable or accurate that *small* disparities should be taken seriously. But if a person turns out to be 15 points or more higher on one scale than on the other (15 points is the standard deviation of the IQ distribution for the Wechsler tests), it may be useful to try to account for this discrepancy and to consider what it may mean in planning the person's future—whether this planning has to do with clinical treatment, educational undertakings, or occupational placement. It is clear, in the first place, that the verbal scale is more closely related to schooling than the performance scale is. A combination of low verbal score and much higher performance score often reflects some educational deficiency. The verbal score also *predicts* far more accurately than the performance score how successful a person is likely to be in future school situations. Besides this difference in the influence of formal schooling, many other factors may be responsible for inequalities between the two halves of the test. When an examiner encounters such a discrepancy, he looks for evidence—in the examinee's record, in what he says, or in what others say about him—that will perhaps account for the discrepancy and will help those who must deal with the person to understand him better. In his report on the person's test results, the examiner regularly includes not just the scores but some qualitative analysis of what the scores may mean.

In general, however, the most valuable information obtained from either the Stanford-Binet or the Wechsler test is an evaluation of over-all intellectual level. Analyses of the correlations between different subtests have shown that a large general factor runs through them all. Binet's belief that intelligence is not the sum of many simpler abilities, but rather as an over-all quality that inheres in various kinds of complex thinking is supported by much research evidence. It is still reasonable to assume that there is such a thing as *general* mental ability, and that we can evaluate it by trying a person out on a variety of questions and tasks. And it is not incompatible with this view to assume that there are also such things as special abilities and talents, but that probably neither the Binet nor the Wechsler test is designed to measure them very efficiently. We shall consider special abilities in more detail in Chapter 5.

We have gone into some detail about the two leading *individual* tests of intelligence because the basic concepts and issues are more clearly defined for them than they are for group tests. But as for frequency of use, group tests rank far ahead of individual tests, millions of them being given each year in schools, in industries, and in military organizations. Thus it is essential that the educated citizen know enough about them to interpret their results intelligently.

Although group intelligence tests are similar in many ways to individual tests, there are some critical differences. Each particular group test is more *limited* in purpose than is an individual test like the Binet or Wechsler. It may be intended for a single age or grade group, for instance, and be inappropriate for children much younger or older. Often related tests for successive age levels are published as a series. There are three Henmon-Nelson Tests, for example, one for Grades 3–6, one for Grades 6–9, and one for Grades 9–12. Group tests differ in types of questions, too. One designed especially for selecting promising college students, such as the Scholastic Aptitude Test of the College Entrance Examination Board, is vastly different in content from a group test designed for sorting out army recruits into various training programs, such as the Army General Classification Test.

Such specificity is an advantage in particular situations. As a rule, an appropriate group test predicts specific criterion scores more successfully than individual tests do. If we wish to know ahead of time the likely first-year grade averages of applicants to a certain college, it would be of no advantage to give each person an individual WAIS test. Scores on the verbal half of this test do predict college grades fairly well, but scores on any one of the special college aptitude tests predict them even better—and the latter can be administered with a fraction of the time and expense involved in individual testing.

What advantages, then, do individual tests have over group tests? First of all, they allow the examiner to get a better idea of how highly motivated the testee is, and to encourage him to put out his greatest efforts. For any one person there is always the possibility that a score on a group test constitutes an extreme underestimate of his ability, if for some reason he was not trying to answer the questions correctly. Secondly, an individual test gives a sounder indication of the mental capacity of a person whose reading skills are not as well developed as his ability to think and reason. Although there are some nonverbal group tests, those most commonly used do penalize nonreaders.

Thirdly, individual tests afford an opportunity for qualitative study and observation. An examiner is more likely to be able to describe the way a child thinks and suggest some possible reasons for his deficiencies after a Wechsler or Stanford-Binet test than after a group test.

A person who knows group tests well has a great variety to choose from. There are extremely difficult tests that challenge the thinking of advanced graduate students and very easy ones suitable for the mentally retarded. There are tests based almost entirely on language and others in which no language of any sort is used either in the items themselves or in the directions. There are tests which yield only a single total score and tests designed to give a differentiated profile of scores. To consider all these types separately would be beyond our concerns here. All we need to note now is that in one way or another they all enable us to compare the general mental ability of an individual with the average of some group to which he belongs or in which he must compete.

INFANT TESTS

One field of research within the general area of intelligence testing deserves special attention because the results obtained are quite untypical. This anomaly is the testing of infants and very young children. All the tests we have been talking about are designed primarily for children of school age and for adults. The Stanford-Binet, which reaches down to a lower age level than the others, does include a group of questions for two-year-olds and has been widely used in preschool testing, but it is not suitable for children younger than two, or even for *dull* two-year-olds. The question inevitably arises: Is it possible to find out how bright a child is before he reaches this age? It would be very helpful for some practical purposes, such as placing children in foster homes, as well as for many research purposes, if such measurements could be made.

There have, in fact, been several well-planned studies of what babies of different ages typically can do. Several infant scales have been developed that enable us to determine how advanced in his development any particular child is. In administering such a test, an examiner may, for example, present a ring to a three-month old baby and observe whether or not he reaches for it. He may listen to the babbling of a nine-month-old to find out whether he can say "da-da" or something equally complex. While the second example would seem to evaluate a rudimentary sort of language development, the largest proportion of the items on infant scales reflect sensori-motor skills.

Such standardized tests of infant development have turned out to be helpful in measuring a child's status *at the time he is tested*. They are useful to pediatricians and others who deal with very young children and who need to be able to base their treatments and recommendations on an infant's developmental age rather than his chronological age. At any age level some children are more advanced than others.

Evidence has piled up, however, that such infant tests do *not* predict how rapid a child's *later* intellectual development will be. The child who is slow about sitting up alone and reaching for objects on the table before him may be the first in his class to learn to read or to master the intricacies of long division. Except for cases of extreme mental retardation, it is not possible to estimate what a child's later IQ is going to be by giving him any sort of test during his first year.

LIMITATIONS AND MISCONCEPTIONS ABOUT INTELLIGENCE

Psychologists have been testing intelligence for many decades now. As we have seen in connection with validity, research and practice with a certain kind of test inevitably lead to changes in our thinking about traits as well as tests. It is not surprising, therefore, that the very definition of intelligence, at least the "intelligence" it has proved feasible to measure, has undergone continuous revision since Binet first formulated his statement about what he was attempting to test. It would be well for all those who are using intelligence tests for one purpose or another to realize that what is measured by such tests is probably a more *limited* human trait than they are assuming.

For there are many things intelligence tests do *not* measure. They cannot give us an over-all index of human *quality,* as some discussions of "giftedness" in children erroneously suggest. They do not get at special talents for art, music, mechanics, or human relationships. They do not tell us how successfully individuals will adapt to new situations.

Neither are they pure measures of *innate* capacity. There are undoubtedly differences among individuals in their hereditary potentialities, but the answers they give to the questions we ask in intelligence tests reflect experience as well as potential, education as well as aptitude. To jump to the conclusion, however, that tests are valueless because they do not measure simply what is given at the beginning of life, and that any order of intellect can be created at will through favorable educational influences, is to disregard large amounts of contrary evidence. For, in fact, at any one time, a score tells us what intellectual development has occurred as a result of some complex mixture of heredity and environment and enables us to say with some assurance what sort of further development to expect under specified conditions. The younger the child is, the more cautious we must be about making remote predictions.

Another misconception that can lead to wrong conclusions about individuals is the assumption that intelligence is a synonym for general learning ability. In the first place, it has been demonstrated rather conclusively that there is no such thing as *general* learning ability. What we find in people are special facilities in learning special things. Thus, one boy quickly learns to throw a baseball; another is inept at ball throwing but quick to develop skill in the use of carpenter's tools. In the second place, scores on intelligence tests are not related to the *rate* at which even school learning takes place. The euphemism "slow learner" is not an accurate way to characterize a dull child. Even when two children have identical MA and IQ scores they may differ widely in the time it takes them to learn how to spell a list of new words or to memorize a multiplication table. Bright children get high marks and move ahead rapidly in school not because they are *faster* at learning the same things everybody else learns, but rather because at each age they are able to grasp more complex, difficult material than their age mates can make sense of. Likewise, the brilliant adult differs from his fellowmen in *what he is able to think about* rather than in how quickly he can learn a new skill or solve a problem. Einstein probably learned no more readily than his fellow citizens how to drive a car or fill out his income tax returns, but he was able to deal with concepts whose complexity was far beyond their scope.

TESTED INTELLIGENCE AS SYMBOLIC THINKING

What all intelligence tests measure is the ability to deal with *symbols*. The more intelligent a person is, the more complex and abstract these symbols can be. As they grow to maturity, children increase their capacity for such symbolic thinking, and they also tend to become specialized in the kind of symbols they can deal with most adequately. Thus, both *level* and *pattern* of intellectual abilities become important considerations. The Wechsler tests, with their separate scores for different kinds of questions, have shown us that any one person is not equally proficient in all varieties of thinking. In the next chapter we shall have more to say about the research that has been done on such inequalities.

Thinking, in which symbols rather than objects themselves are manipulated, is an essential component of civilized life. To be able to measure this capacity, therefore, has been of inestimable value. But let us not assume that it is *all* we need to evaluate in assessing the worth of a person and in helping him to find his place in civilized society.

One special question has, down through the years, been of particular interest to psychologists studying intelligence: What is the nature of the process of mental growth? This problem breaks down into three main subquestions. Is it regular and predictable from early childhood on? (We have already noted that infant test scores do not predict later intellectual level.) At what age does growth cease? (We have already noted that the IQ becomes inappropriate as a measure of intelligence when growth is complete.) Does intelligence change in adult life as a person moves from youth through middle age to senescence? Although there are still some doubtful aspects, research has uncovered fairly satisfactory answers to these three questions. Let us run through the present state of knowledge briefly.

When intelligence tests were new, many studies of large groups of children were made in order to determine whether the IQ, which as we have seen indicates the *rate of growth* characteristic of a child, remains constant from age to age. The answer to the question turned out to be between two extremes, the "constancy" and "anticonstancy" positions. Even after various statistical wrinkles have been ironed out, it is clear that most children show *some* change in IQ during their school years. Shifts up or down of as much as 15 IQ points on the Stanford-Binet test occurred in over half of a group of 40 cases studied over a long period at the University of California. Shifts of 30 or more points occurred in 9 per cent of the cases, and an occasional change of as much as 50 points showed up. Still, the over-all *correlation* between early and later tests from the age of six on is about .80. Thus, we can conclude that it is not likely that a child will appear to be brilliant at one age and retarded at another, or even average at one age and superior at another. As in the case of physical growth, there are some spurts and lapses, but a considerable degree of regularity in the growth rate in most cases. Psychologists and educators have concluded from this research that to be on the safe side they should retest children every few years if they are going to base decisions about such matters as school placement on test scores. An "old" IQ on a child's record should not be used as an indication of his present rate of growth.

The question about when mental growth comes to an end can be answered only by an equivocal "It depends." In the early years of mental testing, when the IQ was the prevailing index of intelligence, test-constructors had to make some decision about the highest chronological age they would use in the denominator for computing IQ's for adolescents and adults. From preliminary observations they decided on 16. But experience with these early scales, such as the 1916 Stanford-Binet, suggested that this figure was too high—that some adolescents were being rated lower in intellectual capacity than they deserved because the denominator of the IQ fraction was too large. Many examiners then shifted to 14, partly influenced by some widely publicized conclusions from the testing of soldiers in World War I that the average intelligence of American citizens was about at that level. But as work with intelligence tests continued, it became apparent that there is no one age at which the ability measured by such tests has ceased growing for everybody. If a test has enough difficult questions to permit increases in ability to show (many of the early tests did not), the average score for students in schools and colleges continues to increase year by year up to the early 20's. Groups of persons not in school, however, do not typically show this increase. Now that accumulated evidence has indicated that education influences what we measure as intelligence, this discrepancy does not seem strange. It is clear, however, that after the middle teens the yearly increases in actual capacity to think in complex abstract terms are *slight* compared with the yearly increases that occur at earlier stages of development. The accumulation of information and the sharpening of the "mental tools" for processing such information can continue throughout life, of course.

Finally, as to the third question, in the early years of the mental-testing movement, comparisons of groups of young, middle-aged, and elderly adults suggested that a decline in intellectual capacity begins almost immediately after its peak is reached. But as *longitudinal* studies of the *same persons* at different stages of life became available, this conclusion was modified. At least through the 40's, slight increases in scores on intelligence tests have been found. Significantly, subjects in these longitudinal studies have been well-educated persons, on the whole. It seems likely, then, that to maintain or improve one's intellectual powers, one must continue intellectual activity. This whole problem will be considered in more detail in Chapter 7.

 With all their faults, intelligence tests are an indispensable tool in modern society. We use them to help us make decisions about the placement of individuals for school and work, and to help us formulate educational and social policies. As research on intelligence tests has continued, they have become sharper and more adaptable. But like all tools they require skillful handling and thorough knowledge of what they will and will not do.

Tests
of Special Ability

Even the most casual observation of people is enough to show us that intelligence is not all that counts toward success. Bill Jenkins does extremely well in college science courses even though he had only an average rating on the intelligence test he took as an entering freshman. But he has studied science and mathematics diligently since he was 12, thereby accumulating a vast amount of specific knowledge and mastering the essential problem-solving skills. Henry Harlow becomes an outstanding machinist because he possesses to an unusual degree the ability to see how parts fit together. Joe McGee shows an amazing

55

5

sensitivity to fine differences in pitch and rhythm and makes use of this talent in learning to play the violin. Lucille Rosen knows far more about contemporary affairs and international relations than anyone else in her high school class and thus becomes the natural candidate to represent her school at an international conference. We could multiply examples of special fitness endlessly.

Psychologists have proceeded along two different lines in developing tests to identify such special talents. These two undertakings, *achievement* testing and *aptitude* testing, at first followed somewhat different courses, but eventually the traffic on the two highways merged. It is still customary for writers on mental testing to distinguish between aptitude and achievement tests, but the distinction has become more a matter of convenience than of basic concepts.

The terms *aptitude* and *achievement* still carry erroneous connotations arising from historical sources. In earlier periods *aptitude* usually meant special talents presumably based on innate, or hereditary, differences among persons rather than on differences due to experience and learning. To say a child had a high degree of musical aptitude meant that he possessed the kind of ear and brain which would facilitate his learning of complex musical skills, not that he possessed some of these skills already. Intelligence, as measured by the tests considered in the previous chapter, was considered to be a special kind of "innate" aptitude for school work. An early book on aptitude testing by Johnson O'Connor was actually entitled *Born That Way*.

Achievement tests, on the other hand, were thought to measure what individuals had *learned*. The search for more reliable and valid achievement tests was stimulated by the demand for better and more convenient school examinations. For in many school situations it is important to obtain an accurate estimate of how much a given student really knows about algebra, English literature, or chemistry. Various special achievement tests were also constructed for nonschool situations, such as trade tests to enable an employment interviewer to find out whether a person claiming to be a skilled worker really belongs in the "skilled" category.

As has already been pointed out, psychologists no longer think intelligence tests measure pure "innate" ability; rather, they measure an unanalyzable mixture of inborn potential and educational experience. This conclusion holds for other varieties of aptitude test. The ability measured by mechanical-aptitude tests, for example, is partly an outgrowth of mechanical experience. The ability measured by clerical-aptitude tests is partly an outgrowth of whatever experiences have sharpened a person's perception of fine details. The ability measured by musical-aptitude tests is partly a reflection of musical training. In practice we cannot disentangle the "natural" from the "acquired" components of aptitude, though we can think about them separately if we like.

Furthermore, in practical studies designed to produce tests of aptitude for particular kinds of work or training, an achievement test often turns out to be the best predictor of later success in the field in question. Thus, tests measuring what a student knows about subjects taught in high school—English, mathematics, science, history, and so on—are used successfully to assess aptitude for college work. A measure of flying information was a valuable part of the test battery used to select Air Force pilots. Spelling tests have been useful in selecting clerical workers.

What then is the distinction between aptitude and achievement tests? Besides the fact that the two varieties of tests have different *histories,* the main distinction is a matter of *purpose.* Tests developed and used primarily to select workers or trainees are labeled aptitude tests. Test developed and used primarily to find out how much students have learned are called achievement tests. The more general term "ability" covers both.

Among the tests we ordinarily classify as aptitude measures are those that resulted from well-known major research programs. A large-scale investigation of mechanical aptitude, at the University of Minnesota, completed in 1930 by Donald G. Paterson and his coworkers, produced three tests that have been in constant use since that time, the Minnesota Spatial Relations Test, the Minnesota Mechanical Assembly Test, and the Minnesota Paper Form Board. At about the same time, another extensive research undertaking at the University of Iowa produced the Seashore Measures of Musical Talents. Other examples could be given, but these two are sufficient to illustrate why certain tests are usually put in the aptitude category today for historical reasons. Other research studies contributed clerical-aptitude tests, methods for identifying artistic talent, measures of dexterity and motor coordination. All such tests have been mainly classed as aptitude rather than achievement measures.

More useful at present, however, than this distinction based on research history is the distinction based on purpose. If we plan to use a test chiefly as a *predictor* of how well individuals will perform in some area, we can consider it an aptitude test, regardless of how its author classified it. If we plan to use it mainly to *evaluate* an individual's accomplishments or the adequacy of his education and experience, it is for our purposes an achievement test, even if its author did not think of it in this way. The two purposes are not exclusive of one another, of course. We may wish to evaluate and to predict for the same person, and the same test may well be useful for both purposes.

VALIDITY FOR DIFFERENT PURPOSES

The advantage of this approach to special abilities lies in clarifying our thinking about the evidence we must have to prove that a test is really valid.

Tests
of Special
Ability

What we are interested in is validity *for specific purposes*. We must make sure that the evidence the author presents for the validity of his test is really relevant to these ends. Just any kind of validity coefficient is not enough. For example, if the author of a test of mechanical comprehension reports that the scores of a group of ninth-grade boys in January correlate to the extent of .65 with independent ratings of these same boys made by their instructor during the same January, we still know nothing about the test's

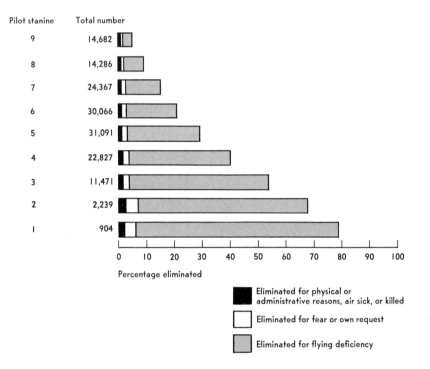

Figure 12. Percentage of candidates eliminated from primary pilot training as related to stanine scores on the selection battery. (Reproduced from Psychological activities in the training command, Army Air Forces, by the Staff, Psychological Section, Fort Worth, Texas, in Psychological Bulletin. *Washington, D. C.: American Psychological Association, Inc., 1945.)*

predictive validity. If our purpose is to select promising students for a technical high school, we need to find some evidence that the test has actually been given to a similar group of boys *before* they entered high school, and that these early scores showed reasonably high correlations with *later* evaluations.

In Figure 12 we see the outcome of a special predictive study of a battery of tests used to select Air Force trainees during World War II. (The stanine is a standard score—"standard nine"—in which 5 is average, one is low, and 9 is high. It is shown along with other derived scores in Figure 8, page 37.) The results turned out to be clear and unambiguous, so that the subsequent use of this set of tests to select pilots was plainly justified. The figures showed that admitting only candidates with high stanines would reduce to a minimum the proportion of men who washed out during primary training.

If we intend to use a test to measure achievement rather than aptitude, a different kind of validity evidence becomes relevant. The main question is whether the *content* of the test really samples the subject matter in question. We can tell something about this by examining the questions. But we also need to get information about *how* the items included in the test were selected and *who* did the selecting. For example, a high school teacher decides to use a standardized achievement test at the end of his course in American history. So he obtains a sample of a test that appears suitable, along with a manual of information about it. If he knows the authors of this test, at least by reputation, and respects their judgment about the objectives of an American history course, he starts out with a favorable attitude. If the manual tells him that a committee of experts drew up the preliminary outline and served as consultants in cases of doubtful items, he is further impressed. If the authors tried out the first set of items on a representative group of students to make sure that the meanings of the questions were clear and that they were neither too hard nor too easy, another point is chalked up in favor of the test.

To summarize, then, an ability test can be considered either an aptitude or an achievement test, depending on the purpose for which we desire to use it. If it is to be used as an aptitude test, *predictive* validity must be demonstrated. If it is to be used as an achievement test, *content* validity is important.

RESEARCH ON SPECIAL ABILITIES

Occupational Studies

Let us turn now to a consideration of what research based on aptitude tests has taught us about the nature of aptitudes, or special talents, themselves. As indicated above, research projects have been set up to explore such general areas as mechanical aptitude, clerical aptitude, motor skill, artistic and musical talent. For a time psychologists held high hopes that it would be possible to identify an appreciable number of special abilities and discover how much of each ability was required for success in each of a considerable number of occupations.

To do so would enable them to do a really "scientific" job of guiding each young person into the occupation for which he was best suited. Unfortunately, as research on the process of occupational choice has progressed, this hope has grown dimmer. Aptitudes, it seems, are more complex, more dependent on special kinds of previous experience, than we first thought they were. Many special talents have turned out not to be measurable at all, at least by present procedures. (Efforts to measure *social* intelligence, for example, have failed). Then, too, interests and abilities often differ widely, so that a person has no wish to enter an occupation in line with his measured aptitudes. Finally, technological change has become so rapid that we have no assurance that a test showing high predictive validity for a particular occupation in 1965 will be related to anything people are doing in 1975.

Factor Analysis

As interest in studying special abilities from the standpoint of occupations has fallen off, research of another kind has increased, namely, a concerted effort to analyze general intelligence into its components and to relate special talents and skills to elements isolated in the analysis. Even though intelligence tests work well and are useful in many situations, psychologists have been increasingly dissatisfied with the idea that we must always be content with a general over-all indication of intellectual capacity. For there are too many instances where a person's intellectual development appears to be very uneven—where he gives brilliant answers to one sort of question but only mediocre ones to another. Accordingly, the idea has drawn a great deal of support that in order to test intelligence adequately, it is necessary to use separate tests for different mental abilities. As we saw in the previous chapter, Wechsler tried to do this, but the abilities measured by the subtests of the WAIS and WISC are not really different enough to produce score profiles from which clear interpretations can be made.

The method psychologists invented for exploring varieties of mental ability is called *factor analysis*. It is a technique for analyzing tables of correlations between test scores so as to illuminate what different tests have in common. Figure 13 illustrates the kind of reasoning involved. Let us suppose that we have given three tests to a large group of high school students. By methods outlined in a previous chapter, we obtain three correlations between scores— for Tests A and B, Tests A and C, and Tests B and C. It turns out that all are positive, but that the correlation between A and C is somewhat lower than the other two. How might we account for this situation? Usually, we assume that there are overlaps in the abilities measured by the three tests and that the correlations reveal how great these overlaps are. The shaded areas in Figure 13 constitute one way of showing this. It is the abilities represented by these areas, abilities which affect one's performance in more than one test, that the factor analyst seeks to locate. The situation with which he actually works is usually a great deal more complicated than that shown in Figure 13. He is more likely to start with 50 tests than with three, and consider simultaneously the 1225 correlation coefficients he obtains from them—$(50 \times 49) \div 2$. After he finds out which ones have something in common, he gives their common "factor" a name based on his analysis of the reasoning, background experience, or special skill that seems to be involved in all the overlapping tests that determine it.

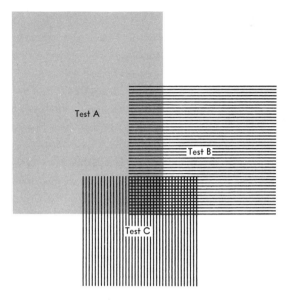

Figure 13. Relationships between what is measured by different tests as postulated by theory underlying factor analysis.

In the early years of factor analysis, there was a good deal of controversy about the conclusions investigators were reaching. Charles E. Spearman held that the most satisfactory inference from analyses of correlations was that all tests measure to varying degrees *one* common factor—what he called "g." Louis L. Thurstone in the 1930's, using more numerous and diverse tests and a more complex method of analysis, concluded that there are from six to ten *primary mental abilities.* He encountered the same pattern of abilities in studies of college students, high school students, elementary school students, and even kindergarten children. He used initials rather than whole words as labels: V (verbal), Q or N (quantitative or numerical), S (spatial), P (perceptual), M (memory), and R (reasoning). In the older groups, a verbal fluency factor he called W (words) seemed to be distinct from the verbal-meaning factor, V, and showed, he felt, more than one variety of reasoning.

Ever more complex factor-analytic studies made during and after World War II have shown that Thurstone's view, like that of Spearman, was an oversimplification. For there are clearly many more varieties of special ability than those listed above, and they are related to one another in highly complex but orderly ways. Both the General Aptitude Test Battery for employment service use, and the Air Force battery mentioned earlier are based partly on factor-analytic methods. J. P. Guilford has concluded that there are at least

120 possible kinds of "testable" ability that can be differentiated from one another in three ways—by the *content* of the test; by the *product,* or form of answer the testee is expected to give; and by the *operation,* or kind of mental process that must be applied to the task given.

One of Guilford's most valuable contributions has been to call our attention to the difference between what he calls *convergent* and *divergent* thinking. Because the questions used in typical intelligence tests have required a subject to give one "right" answer, they measure only convergent thinking. (All the testee's various thoughts must *converge* upon this right answer if he is to succeed). But in life there are many questions to which there is no one right answer. Indeed, some of man's most original thinking is stimulated by such "many-answer" questions. Guilford and his associates have worked out some ingenious techniques for measuring the ability to do divergent thinking. Questions like "Think of as many clever titles as you can for this picture" and "Think of as many uses for a newspaper as you can in two minutes" are examples. These new scales are being widely used in research on creativity and originality.

In using tests constructed by factor-analytic methods, it is important not to attach too much "reality" to the special abilities they appear to measure. *Factors* are essentially just hypotheses about intercorrelations in a battery of tests. Often such hypotheses are very useful aids in thinking about people. But they need to be checked against other information before definite conclusions are drawn.

Cautions in the Use of Special-Ability Tests

Our present thinking about the nature of special aptitudes and talents and about the techniques of constructing tests to measure them projects from both these lines of research—practical prediction studies and theoretical breakdowns of general intelligence by means of factor analysis. Published tests growing out of both branches of research are available for use in schools, personnel offices, and counseling services. It has become increasingly apparent, however, that we must be wary in making inferences from such tests. It no longer seems feasible to try to predict accurately from them how successful an individual is likely to be in a particular line of work. In screening applicants for a job or training program, it is usually necessary to try out the tests we propose to use *in the specific situation,* as correlations between tests and criteria vary widely from place to place. In using aptitude tests to help persons make vocational decisions, too, it is important to use tests that have been tried out in some practical situation so that their relationship to real-life *criteria* is known. Special-ability tests based solely on factor analysis of correlations between *tests* do not tell a person what he needs to know about the way he is likely to perform in a *criterion* situation and thus may lead to unwise decisions.

Sound evidence has piled up that people in different occupations do differ from one another in their special abilities. The average scores for garage mechanics and clerical workers on several tests are shown in Figure 14. Clerical workers, it seems, are well above garage mechanics on educational ability (what is usually called general intelligence), clerical ability as measured by a number-checking test, and three kinds of dexterity. Garage mechanics, however, are higher in both tests of mechanical ability. On the basis of evidence like this it is often possible for a vocational counselor to tell a client whether he has the same pattern of abilities as other people in an occupation he is considering, even if he is not able to predict just how successful the person would be on the job.

A large-scale study by Robert L. Thorndike and Elizabeth P. Hagen reported in the book *10,000 Careers* gives us some additional confirmation that occupational groups do indeed differ in patterns of abilities. It also indicates, however, that the degree of success a person will attain within an occupation cannot be predicted from his test scores. What Thorndike and Hagen did was

Figure 14. Occupational test profiles for clerical workers and garage mechanics. (From: Differential Occupational Ability Patterns *by B. J. Dvorak. Employment Stabilization Research Institute, Vol. 3, No. 8. University of Minnesota Press, Minneapolis. Copyright 1935 by the University of Minnesota.)*

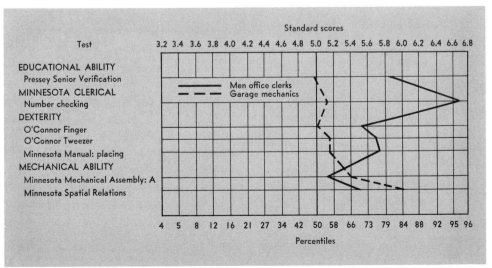

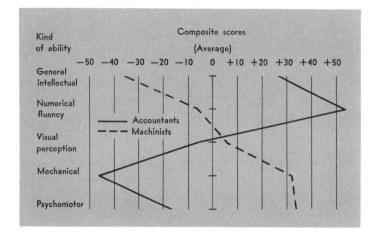

Figure 15. Occupational test profiles for accountants and machinists. (Thorndike, R. L. and Hagen, E. 10,000 careers. *New York: Wiley, 1959, pp. 27–28.)*

first to locate in 1955 as many as possible of the men who had taken the Air Force battery of tests during a certain period in 1943, more than 10,000 in all, and next to find out what occupation each man had gone into. Then they assessed by a variety of methods—such as salary, advancement, professional qualifications—how successful each had been in his work. The profiles of average scores—for different occupational groups—varied widely, as Figure 15 demonstrates. But the correlations between success ratings in the various occupations and scores on the tests were almost all in the near-zero range.

In applying such findings to individual cases, we must remember that the scores plotted in Figures 14 and 15 are *averages*. Within each occupation, individuals vary greatly. Some manage to meet the demands of a job with far less of a given ability than the average worker possesses, others have much more. Since most work can be done in a variety of ways, individuals perhaps use different aptitudes in accomplishing their tasks. This is particularly true of more demanding occupations. However, there are probably limits to this interchangeability, and a worker *too* low on some essential aptitude may not be able to handle a job even if he has many other vocational assets. Thus, a rough sorting process seems to go on constantly in the world of work, one that could produce the patterning we see in Figures 14 and 15.

THE GENERAL APTITUDE TEST BATTERY (GATB)

The goal for the makers and users of vocational aptitude tests should be to facilitate this sorting process, so that it occurs more rapidly, with less waste of time and talents, and with fewer costly mistakes. The task is to identify abilities essential to an ocupation, to construct tests to measure them, and

Tests
of Special
Ability

to set *minimum* scores on each of these tests. Such thinking led to the development of the General Aptitude Test Battery (GATB) by the research staff of the United States Employment Service. In building this set of nine aptitude tests, the researchers used both basic approaches—job analysis leading to tests with predictive validity and factor analysis leading to tests of basic abilities. The nine tests in this two-and-one-half-hour battery measure G (general intelligence), V (verbal ability), N (numerical ability), S (spatial ability), P (form perception), Q (clerical perception), K (motor coordination), F (finger dexterity), and M (manual dexterity). Minimum scores in the critical aptitudes for each particular kind of occupation have been set. Fortunately, the same pattern of essential aptitudes often characterizes a number of related jobs, so the task of interpretation is not unwieldy. With the GATB, an employment counselor can compare an individual's profile with each of 22 Occupational Ability Patterns that have been identified through research. These 22 basic patterns cover more than 500 jobs. Thus, a person who takes the GATB may be made aware of many fields he has never considered, but for which he might qualify. He will also find out if he has less than the minimum amount of some special ability that seems to be required in a type of work he has been considering. For a person thinking about his future, this is a good return on the investment of about two-and-one-half hours of testing time. The GATB shows what can be done when all the knowledge we have accumulated over the years about special vocational aptitudes is brought to bear on one practical problem. Much validity evidence still needs to be collected, however, and the conclusions about a person must be cautious ones. Like all aptitude tests, these are far from infallible.

SPECIAL CHARACTERISTICS AND USES OF ACHIEVEMENT TESTS

Let us look now at some of the facts and principles we need to keep in mind when we use special-ability tests designed to measure achievement—what a person has learned or accomplished.

Essentially, a standardized school achievement test is only a refinement of the examination a teacher gives at the end of a course. Such tests are designed to do accurately and on a large scale what every teacher does routinely when he tries to find out how much of the material of a course each student has mastered. It is no accident that achievement tests have become big business in the United States. Our system of universal public education, secondary as well as primary, brings teachers and school administrators into contact with students drawn from an extremely wide range of home and community backgrounds. Yet because our schools are locally controlled, we have no standard curriculum for the country as a whole, and schools in some areas are far more effective than those elsewhere. Because Americans change residences frequently, children are constantly being shifted from one school system to another. Plainly, some standard way to find out how much an individual child knows about a given school subject is virtually a necessity if we are to make our educational system work. Educational achievement tests, therefore, meet a real social need.

Many of the research procedures we have already discussed have been followed in the production of such batteries of achievement tests as the Iowa Tests of Educational Development (ITED), the Sequential Tests of Educational Progress (STEP), the College Entrance Examination Board tests (CEEB), and the Graduate Record Examination (GRE). But the task of building these tests has some distinctive features. Chief among them is an emphasis on delineating the class of knowledge to be tested *before* starting to construct the test. This is not so easy as it might appear to be at first glance. If you were responsible, for example, for decisions about what should go into the American history test for high school students mentioned earlier (page 59), you would find yourself facing some difficult questions. Should the test be made up of factual questions about names, places, and dates? These are easiest to write and to score, but to most history teachers the transmission of such factual knowledge is not the main purpose of their courses. Should one instead ask questions about historical movements and trends? If so, *which* movements, *which* trends? Historians differ in the emphasis they place on political, economic, and cultural movements; so do textbooks and teachers. Then should an American history test measure the *skills* as well as the knowledge that courses in this subject try to cultivate? Shall we include questions that will enable us to judge how well a student can read and understand historical passages, or how sound his reasoning is when he traces the historical roots of present-day situations and problems?

As suggested before, the most satisfactory way of handling this first step in the construction of an educational achievement test is to set up a committee of competent teachers to discuss the problems and come to some conclusions about what is to be measured. Even though such experts may disagree on details, they can usually reach an agreement about what materials and course objectives are really *basic*. It is this core of fundamental knowledge and skill around which the test should be constructed in order to be appropriate for many classrooms, many schools.

Once this core has been defined and a working outline derived from it, the next major task is to write test items that will be clear, fair, and meaningful. Because the test will be taken by thousands of students whose papers must usually be scored by machine, such items must have one and only one right answer. Furthermore, this answer must not be too easy or obvious if the test is really to serve its purpose of distinguishing among students at many levels of knowledge and proficiency. The writing of good items is an *art*. There are rules for what to do and what not to do, but the skill, like other kinds of writing skill, is not really analyzable.

Once these items have been written, however, and put together in a trial form, statistical techniques are available to help the test-maker decide which ones should be included in the final versions. First he arranges to have several hundred people of the age or class for which the test is intended take the trial form, and he tabulates their responses to each item. From these tabulations he derives indexes of *difficulty* and *discrimination*. As for the former, while it is usually desirable to have a mixture of difficult and easy items in a test, questions which are so easy that almost everybody gets the right answer or so difficult that almost nobody gets it serve no useful purpose. In the final form they are omitted. A discrimination index for an item shows whether students who can be considered to be good at the kind of thinking the test is designed to measure because their over-all score is high are more successful with the item than poor students are. An item that does not discriminate in this way is dead weight in a test. It too is eliminated. It is not uncommon in the course of item analysis of a multiple-choice test to discover that on one particular question good students are actually more likely to choose one of the *wrong* responses than poor students are. Sometimes this happens because they employ a more complex and subtle reasoning than the author of the test anticipated. Naturally, such items are also eliminated before questions are selected for the final form of the test.

Once a satisfactory set of items has been assembled, the rest of the steps in the construction of an achievement test are much like those discussed in Chapter 3. The test-maker must explore reliability, and express it as a reliability coefficient, or standard error of measurement. He must specify standardized procedures for administering and scoring the test. He must work out a meaningful derived score based on a representative sample of the population for which the test is intended. And he must prepare norm tables. As explained previously, if sound decisions about what is to go into the test have been made all along the line, *content* validity is insured.

We have been considering achievement tests from the *producer's* viewpoint. But what does the *consumer*—teacher, school administrator, or the testee himself—need to keep in mind in evaluating these tests and the scores obtained from them? There are so many achievement tests available for measuring what people know about nearly all school subjects at all educational levels that a choice is often difficult. The primary consideration is the one stressed in the preceding paragraphs—content validity. In deciding which of the available batteries of achievement tests to use, for example, a school administrator examines the test and reads very carefully the section in the manual in which the authors explain how the basic outline was developed and how the questions were chosen. If he finds that this task has been done well, he can at least consider the test as a possibility. He will then go on to evaluate its other characteristics—how reliable it is, how convenient it is to administer and score, what the norm groups are like. Perhaps what needs to be stressed most is that to judge the content validity of a test we must do more than examine the test questions themselves. What seems to be a question with a simple factual answer may call for a complex reasoning process. What seems to be an adequate assortment of questions on different principles and concepts may be quite overbalanced in one direction. *Content validity* rests on the whole set of procedures used in planning and constructing the test. *Face validity* alone—what one can judge simply from looking at the questions—is not an adequate basis for choosing a test.

COMBINATION APTITUDE-ACHIEVEMENT BATTERIES

Because there is no clear line separating achievement from aptitude tests, and because special-ability tests of all kinds have turned out to be helpful in schools and counseling offices, *combination* batteries have been worked out for use in educational situations. One group that has been widely used in high schools is called *Differential Aptitude Tests* (DAT). It is composed of eight separate tests—(1) Verbal Reasoning, (2) Numerical Ability, (3) Abstract Reasoning, (4) Space Reasoning, (5) Mechanical Reasoning, (6) Clerical Speed and Accuracy, (7) Spelling, and (8) Sentences. The abilities measured by some of these tests are influenced more by a student's school experience, while the abilities measured by others are affected more by out-of-school experience. The authors and publisher of the battery have collected a large body of information about what one can predict for a student from knowing his scores on these tests. Such predictions may not be so sharp and clear as we might wish—it is not at all certain, for example, that a boy with a high score in Numerical Ability will do better in mathematics courses than a classmate who is high in Verbal Reasoning. But by studying the information the publishers furnish with this test, a teacher or counselor can find out what predictions are possible and how definitely they can be stated. The advantage of a battery of tests of this sort over a single measure of general intelligence is that it is more likely to reveal for each student *some* assets he can count on in planning for his future. The advantage it has over a miscellaneous collection of aptitude and achievement tests is that the norms for all tests are based

**Tests
of Special
Ability**

on the same representative group of people. Thus, the scores that show where an individual stands in relation to this norm population are comparable from test to test, and we can say with assurance, for example, that Hugh ranks much higher in mechanical reasoning than in verbal reasoning.

There are several others of this combination type, and more are likely to become available as time passes. As the search for innate abilities has been abandoned, another question has come into clear focus. What is *useful* to measure about a person in order to facilitate decisions—those that others must make about him and those he must make about his own life? In this vein, it is *useful* to understand what kinds of special ability he possesses, regardless of how this ability was developed. The concept of *special ability,* which emphasizes what can be done with talents rather than where they came from, may gradually take the place of the *aptitude* and *achievement* concepts that have played so important a part in the development of testing methods in the past.

Right now one research undertaking in progress should eventually throw a good deal of light on questions about how special abilities are used. It is called Project TALENT. In the spring of 1960, 440,000 students in 1353 high schools spent two days taking tests. The tests in the TALENT battery had been carefully designed and pretested in order that they might tap as many abilities as possible; 37 separate scores were obtained for each subject. The schools in which testing was done were carefully selected to constitute a complete cross-section of secondary schools in the United States. Besides the test data, many kinds of information were collected about students, schools, and communities. The plan is to follow up these testees in 1961, 1965, 1970, and 1980 to find out what has happened to them—the careers they chose, the education they obtained, their achievements and contributions to society. When the analysis of this formidable body of data is complete, it should tell us more than we have ever known before about what happens to people with different special talents under different circumstances. At each stage of the project, reports are to be published to keep the public informed about what has been learned so far.

The development of special-ability testing has coincided with an increasing awareness by Americans that society as a whole benefits when individuals are encouraged to use their talents effectively and accomplish as much as they can. In this very real sense, what is good for John Jones is good for the country. To the extent that they can help us achieve this joint individual-social purpose, such tests are worth the effort and ingenuity expended on them. Accordingly, they occupy an important position in the total structure of psychological measurement today.

Personality Tests

As we look around us at the people we know—and as we examine our own lives—it is apparent that some of the most distinctive personal qualities cannot be classified as abilities at all. We usually do not know or need to know the score our next-door neighbor makes on a clerical test, but we do find ourselves making some necessary estimate of his friendliness, neatness, cooperativeness, generosity, dependability, and attitudes about politics. Such qualities are essential to the business of living. For success depends on them fully as much as it does on competence. And social problems such

70

6

as crime and mental illness involve faulty personal habits in individuals rather than lack of ability. Clearly, as children grow from infancy to adulthood, emotional maturity is at least as important to develop as intellectual maturity. Thus, it is not strange that psychologists should have taken up the challenge to measure personality traits as well as abilities.

There is some ambiguity about the meaning of "personality test," an ambiguity arising from differences of opinion about how "personality" should be defined. If we take the broad view and define personality as the *total* pattern that includes *all* of a person's characteristics, the tests we have considered in previous chapters would be classed as personality tests. Obviously intelligence, special talents, and achievement in various fields are components of total personality. But it is convenient to consider separately the functions through which a person *uses* these abilities—his motives, emotional stability, interests, adjustment techniques, and the like. To test such qualities we need different techniques from those we use in measuring abilities. One leading author, Lee J. Cronbach, calls them tests of *typical* performance to distinguish them from ability tests, which are tests of *maximum* performance.

The attempt to measure personality characteristics has run into many special difficulties. First of all, the method that worked so well from Binet's time on—placing a testee in a standard situation and obtaining an actual *sample* of his behavior—generally is not applicable here. We simply cannot set up in the testing room the standard situations in which personality traits are most likely to manifest themselves. Many of the most important of these traits are *social* in nature and show up only when an individual finds himself in a certain kind of group. In order really to sample such a trait as self-control, for instance, we would have to standardize situations that were irritating, frustrating, annoying. (Military psychologists tried to do this during World War II by making insulting remarks to persons who were attempting to concentrate on complex psychomotor tasks, but their efforts were not successful. Being insulted by a mental tester is not the same as being insulted by one's superior officer, even though the two situations may look alike.) In ability testing, the use of sample situations is feasible. Problems posed in the testing room can be similar in most essential respects to the problems a person encounters in special situations in life. But in testing personality it is difficult to reproduce the *social* situations in which personality chiefly manifests itself. There has been some challenging research in which this was attempted, but so far no generally usable tests have emerged from it.

The way makers of personality tests have most frequently taken to get around this difficulty is to substitute *reported* behavior for *observed* behavior. Instead of actually trying the testee out to see whether, for example, he becomes angry when someone makes disparaging remarks about him, we ask him to *tell* us how he reacts in such a situation. We include several questions, each dealing with a different specific manifestation of self-control. We obtain a score for him on the trait by counting how many of these manifestations he reports. If there are ten questions on holding one's temper under provocation, the person who says "Yes" to nine of them scores higher in self-control than the person who says "Yes" to only five.

This method of testing personality by asking questions about behavior and feelings in various situations was invented at about the same time as group intelligence tests were. During World War I, Robert S. Woodworth put together a set of questions similar to those psychiatrists ask in screening recruits for emotional stability. This first collection of questions, called the Personal Data Sheet, was the progenitor of a long line of subsequent tests of general adjustment, neuroticism, and other traits related to mental illness and health.

This method—asking a testee to answer questions about his behavior and feelings in life situations—carries with it some testing problems unlike those encountered in ability measurement. The history of personality testing, indeed, can be viewed as a series of efforts to solve these special problems. The most obvious, though perhaps not the most serious, snag is that a person may not tell the truth about himself. In measuring abilities we do not have to worry about this. It is not likely that a boy with an IQ of 90 will be able to "fake" an IQ of 120. Unless his mind works at the 120 level, he is not able to answer the questions so as to attain that score. But it is quite possible for a fearful person to give "brave" answers to questions about his reactions to danger, or for a withdrawn person to say "Yes" to the question, "Do you have many friends?" If a person's suitability for a job, a college, or an exclusive club is to be judged on the basis of his personality test scores, he is under a real temptation to "fake good."

Military psychologists also found out that at times a person may be tempted to "fake bad." Some draftees who showed what looked like serious psychiatric disabilities on the initial screening test were adjudged quite healthy when more penetrating methods of examining them were employed. They had hoped to be classified neurotic and answered the questions toward that end.

Fortunately, psychologists have devised ways of discovering whether answers have been faked, so a score can be either discarded or corrected for deception. We shall mention some of these devices later in the chapter. Here we can simply note this difficulty as one of the special complications encountered in personality testing.

Another obstacle has turned out to be even more difficult to surmount. A person is often *unable* to describe his own motives and emotional characteristics honestly even if he wishes and intends to do so. As Freud made us aware, a large part of our motivation is unconscious. And the pull of unconscious wishes distorts a person's view of his own personality. The man with strong dependent needs often sees himself as an aggressive, self-reliant individualist. The woman with a powerful undercurrent of hostility in her relations with her family may see herself as gentle and self-sacrificing. Thus, any score may not mean what it seems to mean.

Fortunately enough, some of the characteristics people unconsciously express in their answers to test questions are common to many testees, and are therefore measurable. Various kinds of such *response sets* have been identified. Allen L. Edwards studied one of these in detail, a set he called *social desirability*. He found that since persons who grow up in our society almost inevitably learn what is considered to be the "right" way of behaving and feeling, the answers they give on any kind of personality inventory reflect their response to this awareness, perhaps more than they reflect actual emotional characteristics. A second response set that influences personality test scores is *acquiescence,* that is, the tendency to agree with what someone else says, to answer "Yes" rather than "No." Still another response set that has been explored is *deviance,* or the tendency to give unusual or uncommon answers to personality questions. It is clear, then, that we cannot automatically take personality scores at their face value. We must have some way to control or to make allowances for the other tendencies, besides out-and-out faking, that influence these scores.

Another, rather different, difficulty psychologists have run into in devising personality tests has been the lack of unambiguous criteria for evaluating test validity. As we have seen, one standard method for validating ability tests is to correlate test scores with nontest indicators of the trait measured. The tradition began with intelligence tests. Binet took it for granted that the trait he was trying to measure was the same as the trait teachers observed in their bright, average, and dull students. Thus, he could find out whether his tests were measuring this characteristic by correlating test scores with teacher judgments, as expressed in school marks, promotions, and the like.

In the case of most of the personality qualities we might wish to measure, however, it is difficult to obtain criterion measures from life. We can, of course, ask people to rate their students, employees, fraternity brothers, or neighbors for optimism, dependability, or general adjustment. But such ratings are unsatisfactory in many ways as measures of personality. First, raters often disagree markedly in their evaluation of the same person, reflecting their own attitudes perhaps as much as the characteristics of the person they are rating. Second, ratings show what is usually called a "halo" effect—that is, a person who elicits generally favorable attitudes tends to receive high ratings on everything; a person not generally liked is rated low on everything. Furthermore, it is difficult to persuade raters to spread their judgments over a range of numbers; if the rating scale runs from 1 to 9, they hesitate to give anyone a "1" or a "9" and may rate everybody "5," "6," or "7." Had ratings been more satisfactory as a way of measuring personality, perhaps there would not have been as much pressure to develop personality tests themselves. Ratings are still widely used, though, both for evaluating personality in practical situations and for exploring the relationships of personality tests to other measures. One does not discard a dull tool until a sharper one is available. But in interpreting ratings we must always take their deficiencies into consideration. They are not really satisfactory criteria for personality tests.

One way of investigating the validity of personality tests is to compare defined groups of people singled out by society on the basis of some trait. This method has been particularly useful in research on neurotic and psychotic tendencies, for the extremely maladjusted are likely to show up eventually for psychiatric treatment. Assuming that there is an underlying continuum of adjustment and that psychiatric patients as a group represent one end of it, then evidence that they obtain extreme scores on an adjustment inventory becomes evidence for the validity of the test. (This is an oversimplification. There are several *kinds* of maladjustment represented by groups with different psychiatric diagnoses, so that not one but a number of traits must be assumed. But the same reasoning applies to the complex situation.)

The availability of clearly defined groups to facilitate the validation of adjustment-maladjustment tests has stimulated research in this particular area. It has been stimulated also by the demand for tests in mental hospitals and clinics. This concentration of research efforts has resulted in many more tests for *negative* than for *positive* personality traits.

It is much easier to discover, for example, that Lawrence Wylie has a strong undercurrent of anxiety, a tendency toward paranoid thinking, and more than the usual number of psychosomatic symptoms than it is to assess his dependability, loyalty, and leadership potential. We must always keep in mind this bias of personality measurement toward the negative rather than the positive side whenever we use personality tests.

To some extent, this negative bias is being corrected as research continues. In one area, the measurement of vocational interest, E. K. Strong was able to capitalize on the existence of occupational groups in constructing the Strong Vocational Interest Blank, a valuable test for measuring motivations that determine life decisions. In another large research program, David C. McClelland and others tackled the *achievement motive* and devised ways of measuring it. We shall have more to say about these particular tests later. Here they serve only as examples of a trend in research that will eventually round out the field of personality measurement so that we can assess favorable traits as adequately as unfavorable traits.

CLASSIFICATION OF PERSONALITY TESTS

By Traits Measured

What personality traits can be measured by tests? It is not possible to answer this question completely, for literally hundreds of tests are available, and in many cases it is not clear just what they do measure. We can, however, outline some main headings under which most of the titles would fall. There are, first of all, many tests of what we label *"general adjustment"* or *"emotional stability,"* though it would probably be more accurate to call them measures of *mal*adjustment, *in*stability, or neuroticism, since they are made up of questions related to mental illness. Although their usefulness varies from situation to situation, evidence is abundant that tests of this sort often help in the diagnosis of what might be called *vulnerability to psychiatric difficulties.* The second main group of personality tests, overlapping to some extent with the first, consists of measures of *social or unsocial tendencies.* Here again it is the difficulties in social relationships that such tests show up most clearly. So far, ways to measure unusual social sensitivity or real talent for social relationships have eluded us. A third group of tests, sharing common ground with both of the first two types, consists of measures of *motives,* or basic *needs.* A fourth and much smaller group consists of measures of *values.* A fifth variety, developed quite independently of the others, is *vocational interest* tests. A sixth variety is composed of *attitude* scales. These include measures of interpersonal attitudes as well as approaches toward things and issues.

In addition to these main classes, we would have to provide a large miscellaneous category to do justice to the enormous amount of exploratory research that has occurred. Varieties of temperament, character traits, psychosexual characteristics, ways of dealing with frustration, defense mechanisms, reactions to authority—for these and many other aspects of personality measurement techniques have been devised. But for most of these qualities we do not as yet have tests that are ready to be used in *practical,* as distinguished from *research,* situations. Browsing through psychological journals of the last two or three decades, we can find a test for almost any trait we can think of (and probably for a good many others we haven't). While only a comparatively small number of these have accumulated enough evidence about what they measure and where they are applicable to be considered for most purposes, they chart promising directions for future development.

By Technique, or Method

Instead of classifying personality tests according to *what* they measure, we can classify them according to *how* they measure. There are two large classes here—the inventories and the projective techniques. So far we have been talking mainly about tests of the inventory type, in which the respondent answers questions about his typical behavior or describes his feelings about objects, situations, or people. But in the other family of personality tests, the *projective techniques,* subjects respond to ambiguous stimuli, such as inkblots or pictures. This class has become increasingly popular, both in research and in practical assessment. Here, too, besides these two main types, we must acknowledge a large miscellaneous category—objective performance tests, physiological measures such as electroencephalograph or galvanic skin response, situational tests, and many others. But the inventories and the projective tests are the tools psychologists are most likely to use in clinics, schools, and consulting offices.

It is not possible for us to consider here even a small fraction of the large number of specific tests. What we can do, though, is to look closely at some of the more prominent specimens in these major classes. Let us first consider a questionnaire-type test originally constructed to measure tendencies toward various kinds of psychiatric difficulties, the *Minnesota Multiphasic Personality Inventory* (MMPI).

PERSONALITY QUESTIONNAIRES

The MMPI

The characteristic that sets the MMPI apart from most of the other tests of maladjustment is the *empirical* method by which its scoring keys were constructed—that is, the authors used *experience* with the items in each scale rather than theory or common sense in deciding how they should be scored. Starting with a large collection of 550 questions about feelings, attitudes, and symptoms, they asked clear-cut diagnostic groups of psychiatric patients to answer the questions. Another group of men and women, similar to the psychiatric patients in age and social class but not mentally ill, answered the same questions. The authors then carefully tabulated the answers each group gave to each of the 550 questions. Only the items that had a clear, statistically significant difference in frequency of response between psychiatric and normal groups were scored as indicators of the psychiatric trend. For example, a response is scored on the scale for *Paranoia* only if paranoid patients give it more frequently than normal persons do.

To proceed in this empirical way is to by-pass some of the persistent problems discussed in the previous pages. Instead of having to struggle with the question, "Is the person really telling us the truth about his attitudes and behavior?" we shift our position and say instead: "His answer to this question is a bit of verbal behavior in its own right. Let's see if we can find out what it is related to." We search for behavioral correlates of what persons *say* about themselves, and give up the essentially unanswerable question about whether consciously or unconsciously, they are telling the "truth."

For the MMPI, nine scales have been constructed in this manner to measure tendencies toward different kinds of psychiatric difficulty. In the course of various research projects, psychologists have added a number of other scales based on other nonpsychiatric group comparisons, such as introverts versus extraverts, and prejudiced versus unprejudiced. The experience clinicians in hundreds of agencies have had with the test has resulted in the accumulation of an appreciable amount of practical knowledge about the meaning of different combinations of high and low scores. These combinations, or profiles, of scores have turned out to be of more value than any of the single scores. A schizophrenic patient, for instance, may not score any higher on the Sc (schizophrenia) scale than a neurotic patient does, but his pattern of scores is distinctive enough so that a skilled interpreter can get useful information about him from examining this profile. Figure 16 on page 78 shows such a profile and the inferences on personality a clinician can draw from it.

Besides developing the regular scoring keys, they worked out several special keys to help the interpreter correct for faking and unconscious response sets. The method for detecting faking happily is applicable to many other tests as well as the MMPI. Essentially rather simple—a direct extension, in fact, of the empirical method by means of which the personality scales themselves were constructed—it employs item analysis. The general procedure is to ask a group of subjects to take the test twice—once under standard instructions and once under instructions to bias their scores. They might be told, for example: "Answer the questions in such a way as to make as favorable a score as possible." Item by item, responses given under the two conditions are tabulated. When the proportions are compared, differences on

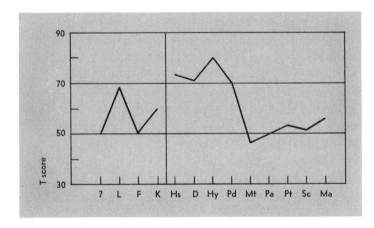

Figure 16. An MMPI profile. From such a record, a psychologist would suspect that the testee was not entirely honest in his responses (high L and moderately high K scores), was neurotic rather than psychotic (high Hs, D, and Hy, with average Pa, Sc, and Ma), and was suffering from psychosomatic symptoms (high Hs and Hy).

some items are statistically significant. These items are used in the special "fake good" key.

The procedure outlined above was one of the sources of items in the K scale of the MMPI. A high K score thus may indicate defensiveness or unwillingness to admit one's personal weaknesses. A low K score may indicate excessive self-criticism or a deliberate attempt to "fake bad." It is always necessary to analyze what high and low K scores *may* mean in individual cases, however. A person with an unusually high K score may not be *faking* good. He may really *be* good!

The MMPI has other special scales designed for special purposes. The F scale, for example, consists of answers very rarely given by anybody. If a person comes out with a high score on the F scale, there is a possibility that he is a highly original individual who sees things differently from the average man. There is also a possibility that he is psychotic. But it is far more likely that something went wrong with the test in his case—perhaps that he got confused about the instructions or placed his answers opposite the wrong numbers on the answer sheet. A high F score is a signal to the psychologist that he should not pay too much attention to the other scores on a test profile until he makes sure that the marks on the paper really represent what the person meant to say in answer to the questions. The L score is made up of a group of questions about such highly favorable characteristics that a person who is telling the truth will rarely say "yes" to them. It measures a less subtle kind of deception than K.

The Strong Vocational Interest Blank (SVIB)

The Strong blank is also an empirically scored inventory. Its history is considerably longer than that of the MMPI. Soon after World War I, E. K. Strong and some other psychologists studying occupational differences happened upon an interesting fact—

that different groups of professional people showed consistent differences in what they said they liked and disliked. Some of these differences were what common sense would have predicted. It is natural that more engineers than salesmen should say that they like physics, for example. But significant differences also turned up on items having no apparent connection with jobs—items concerned with amusements, hobbies, people, books, and many other aspects of life. Such findings suggested that a profession may represent a way of life as well as a way of earning a living. Strong saw that it would be possible to measure these characteristics related to occupational choice. In a systematic program of research extending over many years, he worked with men from one occupational group after another, comparing the responses they gave to the test questions with the responses given by men in general. In constructing a scoring key for the Architect scale, for example, he asked several hundred practicing architects to take the test. Item by item, he tabulated their answers to find out which ones they answered "Like," which "Indifferent," and which "Dislike." Any answer for which the difference between architects and men in general was statistically significant was included in the Architect scoring key. Later, Strong devised a special form of the test for women, and developed scales for women's occupations in the same way. Norms for all the occupational groups studied were provided, and the relationship of interest scores to age, special abilities, and many other human characteristics were explored. In its present form, the Strong Vocational Interest Blank for Men consists of 400 items drawn from several areas of life—occupations, school subjects, amusements, kinds of people, work situations, and so on. The Strong Vocational Interest Blank for Women consists of some of the same items, along with others that are more characteristic of what women do in our society. There are 45 occupational keys for the men's blank, 26 for the women's blank. Thus a young person who takes one of these tests receives, in one package, a large amount of information about whether or not he would be likely to feel that he fits in or belongs in one of these lines of work. In Figure 17 on page 80 we see a Strong profile and what the person who obtained it could conclude about himself.

With the SVIB, as with the MMPI, the empirical approach has yielded supplementary keys for scoring other things besides the occupational characteristics the test is specially designed to measure. From comparing item tabulations of boys of 15 and men of 25 or over, an *Interest Maturity* key took shape. Comparing men's responses with women's produced the *Masculinity-Femininity* key. As with the occupational scales, we know what an individual's score on one of these keys means if we are aware of how it was constructed. For example, when a college freshman scores in the bottom quarter of his group on Interest Maturity, we know that at present he is more

Report on Vocational Interest Test for Men

Name .... Age .... Date .... Agency or school .... Case no. ....

Group	Occupation	Raw Score	Standard Score	C						B—	B	B+	A				
				0	5	10	15	20	25	30	35	40	45	50	55	60	65
I	Artist																
	Psychologist (rev.)																
	Architect																
	Physician (rev.)																
	Psychiatrist																
	Osteopath																
	Dentist																
	Veterinarian																
II	Physicist																
	Chemist																
	Mathematician																
	Engineer																
III	Production Manager																
IV	Farmer																
	Carpenter																
	Printer																
	Math. Sci. Teacher																
	Policeman																
	Forest Service																
	Army Officer																
	Aviator																
V	Y.M.C.A. Phys. Dir.																
	Personnel Manager																
	Public Administrator																
	Vocational Counselor																
	Y.M.C.A. Secretary																
	Soc. Sci. Teacher																
	City School Supt.																
	Minister																
VI	Musician																
VII	C.P.A. Partner																
VIII	Senior C.P.A.																
	Junior Accountant																
	Office Worker																
	Purchasing Agent																
	Banker																
	Mortician																
	Pharmacist																
IX	Sales Manager																
	Real Estate Slsmn.																
	Life Insurance Slsmn.																
X	Advertising Man																
	Lawyer																
	Author-Journalist																
XI	President																
	Occupational Level																
	Masculinity-Femininity																
	Specialization Level																
	Interest Maturity																

Figure 17. Profile of scores made by an 18-year-old college student on the Strong Vocational Interest Blank. While the A and B+ scores suggested a number of career possibilities, the combination of Physician, Chemist, and Engineer with Artist, Musician, and Author, along with the A on Architect, made Architecture appear to be the most promising choice, since it combines scientific and artistic interests. The young man entered an architecture course and did well with it. (Reprinted from Manual for Strong Vocational Interest Blanks for Men and Women *by E. K. Strong, Jr., with the permission of Stanford University Press, © Copyright 1959.)*

like a boy than a man. But we cannot predict from Interest Maturity score alone how likely he is to grow up in his interest pattern as he proceeds through college. Some men, after all, remain "boyish" all their lives.

On the basis of extensive research extending over more than three decades we know a number of things about vocational interests, as measured by the Strong blank. First, patterns of likes and dislikes are not primarily the result of participation in an occupation, but exist *before* a person enters it. For example, Stanford students who were later to enter medical school and become physicians, scored high on Strong's *Physician* scale even in their undergraduate days. Most people, it seems, develop their individual interest patterns before their high school days are over.

Second, for most persons, such interest patterns, once set, are as stable and permanent as any aspect of personality that has been studied. Strong kept in touch with many of the Stanford students he tested in the 1930's and from time to time he wrote to them and asked them to take the test again, so that he could find out whether they had changed. Although he did usually find minor changes, and although a few individuals showed completely altered interest pictures at different times, the great majority did not change substantially over periods as long as 22 years.

Long-term research has also revealed a great deal about what Strong scores do and do not predict. With a few exceptions such scores do *not* tell us just how successful a person is likely to be in an occupation or in the training program leading to it. (Perhaps we should never have expected that they would. An individual score expresses how much a person resembles an occupational group made up entirely of men successful enough to stay in the field. Degrees of success are not considered.) What the scores *do* predict is how likely individuals are to remain in particular occupations or shift to others. Further, although some studies indicate that the correlation between interest scores and self-rated job satisfaction is not very high, evidence suggests that those who are in occupations on which they obtained high Strong scores are on the whole better satisfied with their positions than are others whose interest scores did not point in the particular direction they took.

Other Personality Inventories

We have discussed the MMPI and the Strong tests as outstanding examples of what the inventory, or questionnaire, approach to personality measurement has accomplished. They are tests in which at least some of the special measurement problems we considered at the beginning of the chapter have been solved by selecting items that differentiate between groups already sorted out by society—for instance, Schizophrenics versus Normals, or Dentists versus Men-in-General. But there are other tests representing this same approach to measurement problems. The California Psychological Inventory, for example, is similar to the MMPI in many ways, but the questions of which it is composed have nothing to do with psychiatric illness, and the special groups on whose responses the scoring keys are based are normal people—high-achieving and low-achieving students, for example. This test represents a forward step in the direction of measuring positive characteristics of people rather than just symptoms and deficiencies.

Besides the empirical approach there are other question-and-answer routes to personality measurement. One way is to explore through correlational methods the associations between items in a given test. If it is discovered, for instance, that of 500 people who have taken the test most of the persons who answer "Yes" to the first question also answer "Yes" to questions 5, 8, 19, 20, and 23 and "No" to questions 3, 11, and 17, then these clusters of items appear to have something in common. The test-maker asks himself, "What is it?" Often he can tell simply from reading the items themselves. The next step is to isolate this little cluster of items and make a separate scale of it, perhaps adding other items that appear to be similar in order to make it more reliable. An example of a test constructed in this way is the Guilford-Zimmerman Temperament Survey with its separate scales for General Activity, Restraint, Ascendance, Sociability, Emotional Stability, Objectivity, Friendliness, Thoughtfulness, Personal Relations, and Masculinity. Another example is the Kuder Preference Record for measuring interests. In using tests of this type we must always remember that each score measures what a person *says* about himself, not necessarily the way he acts; we cannot assume the latter unless validation studies in real-life situations have been conducted. In the case of the Kuder Preference Record, for one, there has been a considerable amount of such checking up on what persons with various kinds of scores actually do. Clearcut and stable occupational differences, for example, have been found.

Another general approach to the problem of measuring personality characterizes researchers who start with a personality *theory* and then work from it in deciding what traits to measure and what questions to ask pertinent to those traits. This was how most projective tests began (see pages 84–87). But it has often been used as an approach to paper-and-pencil tests also. One example is the *Edwards Personal Preference Schedule* (EPPS), designed by Allen Edwards to measure the strength of 15 of the personality needs postulated by Henry A. Murray in *Explorations in Personality,* needs like Achievement, Affiliation, and Order. In using such a test in practical situations we must remember that personality theories themselves have not been "validated." Therefore, we must be on guard against making inferences about what an individual scoring high in a certain trait is likely to *do* in an actual situation unless we have some definite evidence that the trait in question really shows up in such situations. To hire a secretary simply because she scores high on "Need for Order" as measured by EPPS, for example, might be a mistake. We are not really sure that there is such a trait as "Need for Order," and even if it exists, we are not sure how it would be expressed in our particular office. It might make its possessor so intolerant of necessary confusion that she would make life miserable for herself, her fellow workers, and her boss.

The Edwards Personal Preference Schedule illustrates another aspect of personality testing that has taken on great importance in current work. As mentioned before, Edwards has collected a large amount of evidence which indicates that the answers people give to personality questions are often largely determined by a conscious or unconscious effort to present a *socially desirable* picture of themselves. In order to rule out the effects of this tendency, Edwards gave a preliminary try-out to all the questions he intended to use in the test.

He asked his guinea pigs to evaluate the social desirability (SD) of each of the answers to each question. (Previous research had shown that people could make such evaluations, and that the SD ratings were stable from group to group and from time to time.) Then as he built his test, he put together pairs of items with similar SD ratings. The testee is required to choose one or the other in each case, rather than just to say "Agree" or "Disagree" to each of them. Thus, a high "Need for Achievement" score on the EPPS shows that the person chose as descriptive of himself many statements about achievement, even when he had to pass up statements about equally admirable qualities. This method of presenting items, usually called *forced-choice,* has been used by various psychologists, in rating scales as well as in self-descriptive inventories.

Flourishing research aimed at overcoming other response sets, such as those discussed earlier in the chapter, is widespread. As a result, it is now possible to make direct measurements of the tendencies to answer "Yes" rather than "No" to questions, to give deviant rather than common answers, and to take extreme rather than moderate positions when asked how strongly one agrees or disagrees with various statements. Personality testing by questionnaire has definitely come a long way since Woodworth proposed his Personal Data Sheet in 1918.

Let us turn now to the other main branch of personality testing, the projective methods. With these, instead of asking the testee questions, the examiner presents to him some ambiguous stimulus and asks him to interpret it or react to it. Inkblots and pictures of human situations have been the most common stimuli used. For example, see Figures 18 and 19. Since an inkblot is not really a picture of anything, the interpretation a person gives must come from within himself and thus express something about the way he perceives and organizes his individual world. Similarly, since the picture in Figure 19 does not make it clear what the two persons are doing or saying to one another, any story a person makes up about it must stem from his own thoughts and feelings. This suggests the reason for the label of this type of test: The testee is said to *project* into the picture his own emotional attitudes and ideas about life. Some have argued that *self-expressive* would be a better over-all designation for these methods, but the title *projective* is old, and it has stuck.

Figure 18. Inkblot Number 7 in the Rorschach series. (Hans Huber Publishers.)

The first of these tests to be widely used, and still probably the most popular of them all, is the Rorschach test. This is a set of ten inkblots of various shapes. Some are black and white only, some have color as well. The subject is asked to tell what he sees in each one. After he has said as much as he wishes to say, the examiner asks as many questions as are needed to make clear just what the subject saw in the blot and what aspect of it determined his perceptions. Since 1921 when Hermann Rorschach, a Swiss psychiatrist, proposed this technique, a number of somewhat different scoring systems have been developed, and a tremendous number of books and journal articles have been written about it. The various scoring systems provide for separate analysis c

Figure 19. A picture similar to those used in projective personality tests. (Photo courtesy Standard Oil Company of New Jersey.)

the structure, or style, of the responses and of their content. *Structure* has to do with such questions as: How productive is the person in responding to this sort of stimulus? In other words, does he have many responses or few to each card? Does he usually react to each figure as a whole or to its parts? To what extent does he base his responses on form, color, and shading? *Content* pertains to the extent to which he sees the blots as human figures, animals, anatomical diagrams, maps, clouds, or other concrete things. The degree to which a person tends to give either popular or original responses is also of some interest.

It should be evident from even this brief description of the many aspects to analyze in an individual's responses to inkblots that the job of interpretation is a highly complex undertaking. For one thing, there is no way in which a test like this can be validated all at once. As research studies have accumulated over the years, it has become apparent that a good many of the inferences clinicians were once accustomed to make on the basis of this test were unjustified. It has not proved to be the "Open Sesame" to personality secrets that its more enthusiastic practitioners thought it was going to be. But in spite of its inadequacies it is still a valuable tool for practicing clinicians. Used along with other techniques for assessing personality, such as interviews and background information, it furnishes clues about matters that can profitably be explored in studying an individual case. The Holtzman Ink Blots, brought out in 1961, correct some of the deficiencies of the Rorschach technique while keeping many of its advantages.

Another widely used projective technique is the Thematic Apperception Test (TAT). It consists of cards showing pictures of people. What the situation is in each case and how the persons are feeling about it are purposely left undefined so that the testee can have an opportunity to read in his own attitudes and ways of perceiving the world. His task is to make up a story for each picture, including in his account some explanation of what led up to the illustrated situation, what the characters are thinking and feeling, and what the outcome will be. Figure 19 shows a picture similar to those used in the TAT.

As with the Rorschach, many ways of analyzing and interpreting a person's TAT stories have been explored. Generally, though, the examiner looks first to see which character has been made the protagonist of the story, since that is probably the person with whom the story-teller identifies. He then studies the details of each story carefully—what the subject said and how he said it— deriving hypotheses therefrom about the individual's needs, feelings, and attitudes, and noting how often the same trends occur in different stories. Most clinicians use this information as a basis for a verbal description of the testee rather than a score or set of scores. Researchers, however, give over-all ratings for the personality traits in which they are interested.

The research possibilities in this general method have been exploited in many ways. Special sets of pictures for children, Negroes, and persons from other cultures have been tried. Methods of scoring for specific characteristics have been standardized. A good example of the use of the story-telling method in research is the work of McClelland and his associates on *achievement* motivation, to which we referred earlier (see page 75). They presented to their research subjects pictures carefully selected to stimulate the invention of stories about achievement. Then they analyzed each person's stories according to a standardized system. They considered the desires the main character expresses, the activity he engages in, and the obstacles he encounters, along with several other features. Thus, they obtained a score for each subject on Need Achievement. In a continuing program of research they have been studying the ways in which these scores relate to the people's backgrounds and subsequent achievements.

We could mention many other particular varieties of projective tests, but any complete discussion would carry us far beyond our present interests. One thing we can say of all the projective tests: Their validation is incomplete. They are not therefore ready to be applied in making decisions about people in practical situations as teachers, social workers, and employment managers must do. In the hands of a competent psychologist with a wide background of knowledge about personality structure and functioning, they can often contribute to such decisions. But there is no way in which a person can attain skill in the use of projective tests without this background of psychological knowledge. The taking of a single course in Projective Techniques certainly does not provide it.

Perhaps the greatest value of projective techniques lies in the contribution they make to research on personality. For they allow psychologists to get some clues about things people are not able to talk about directly—their underlying motives, assumptions, and ways of looking at the world.

MISCELLANEOUS WAYS OF ASSESSING PERSONALITY

In addition to these two principal kinds of personality measures, inventories and projective techniques, there are some direct methods of evaluating personality, methods that have been in use for centuries and are still used today. These are observation, interviews, and ratings, all of which, it has been repeatedly demonstrated, have serious weaknesses. Mainly they arise because such methods involve observers, and the personality of the *observer* plays at least as great a part as the personality of the *observed* in the final product. We see this in everyday life. Two bystanders witness the same automobile accident and tell different stories about what the driver of the car actually did. Two interviewers talk to the same applicant and come out with widely different assessments of his competence and attractiveness. Two English teachers read the same theme; one marks it A, the other D.

We could multiply instances of this kind indefinitely. But it would be unwise to conclude that we should never use such evaluations of personality. There are too many situations in which they are the only possible methods by which we can get some information about personal qualities. No tests are available, for example, that will tell a school superintendent whether a teacher he is thinking of hiring has the necessary characteristics for stimulating students in a classroom. Repeated efforts have been made to develop personality tests of the qualities good teachers show, but they have been only partially successful. Thus, the superintendent must rely on letters of recommendation and interviews in making his evaluations.

There are many other situations where, unless or until better personality tests become available, ratings, observations, interviews, and letters of recommendation will continue to be employed. Earlier in this chapter we discussed some of the inadequacies of ratings as criteria for personality tests. Clearly, if it is necessary to use rating scales to assess personality traits not otherwise measurable, we must give some attention to remedying these defects. Discrepancies between raters will be less troublesome if we make it a practice to secure several raters and use the *average* of their judgments. Clear instructions about just what is to be rated also help. Judges can be forced to distribute their ratings over a wide range rather than to mark everybody "average" or "above average" by asking them to *rank* the individuals to be evaluated or to divide them into, say, five groups each made up of a specified number of people. Or the forced-choice method we have explained when discussing the Edwards Personal Preference Schedule can be used for ratings as well as for self-reports. In the teacher-rating problem mentioned above, for example, one item to be rated by the supervisor who has been in charge of a student's practice teaching might be:

> In which of these ways is the applicant *more* competent?
> Writes clear detailed lesson plans.
> Wins confidence of his class.

Both of these qualities are socially desirable but one is probably more fundamental to success as a teacher than the other is. To construct such a forced-choice scale, of course, we must first collect a great deal of information both about the actual social desirability of certain kinds of behavior and about traits that are really related to success at a particular task. Developing any kind of good rating scale is not easy.

Although psychologists have devoted more attention to rating scales than to the other miscellaneous ways of obtaining information about personality, they have done some research on observations, interviews, application blanks, and recommendations. The purpose, of course, has been to increase the accuracy of these techniques and to get rid of some of the sources of ambiguity and error. One way of doing this is to clarify the instructions given to observers, interviewers, and persons filling out application blanks. Another is to analyze which observations, which questions, and which answers show predictive validity for some particular criterion. Personnel psychologists have found ways to score the answers applicants for a certain position give—prospective insurance salesmen, for example—by using tabulations of the answers given by successful and unsuccessful workers previously hired.

Behavior observations of many sorts still constitute an indispensable source of information about personal qualities. It seems unlikely that testing techniques will ever replace them completely.

Applications of Tests and Measurements

Every day thousands of decisions are made that rest at least partly on evaluations of a person's psychological characteristics. Some are decisions *about* people, as when an employment manager selects a new man for a job, or the staff of a mental health clinic plans the treatment of a new patient. Some are decisions *by* people, as when Jerry makes up his mind that he will enter graduate school instead of taking a job as a petroleum geologist, or Beverly shifts her major from biology to political science. In any of these situations, a well-chosen test in the hands of someone who understands it may be of enormous value.

89

7

When the decision involves the selection of one or more individuals from among a group of applicants, the contribution a test makes can be analyzed in a simple straightforward way. Whether the selection is for a college, for a job, or for a therapy group, the purpose of the decision-maker is to pick out people who will *fit* into the place he has in mind for them. He does not expect to be right every time, only most of the time—he wants to select more successes than failures. Tests can sometimes improve his batting average even if their reliability and predictive validity are not especially high. Consider, for example, the expectancy table shown in Table 6. If the person who does the hiring selects

TABLE 6

How a Stenographic Proficiency Test Can Contribute to the Selection of Good Stenographers

Number in each score group receiving each rating on stenographic ability				Stenographic Proficiency Test Scores	Percentage in each rating group that fall in each score group			
Below Average	Average	Above Average	Excellent		Below Average	Average	Above Average	Excellent
	4	6	7	18–19		17	40	64
	2	2	4	16–17		9	13	36
	10	5		14–15		44	33	
	4	1		12–13		17	7	
2	2	1		10–11	67	9	7	
1	1			8–9	33	4		
3	23	15	11		100	100	100	100

This expectancy table shows the number and percentage of stenographers of various rated abilities who came from specified score groups on the *S-B Stenographic Proficiency Test*. ($N = 52$, mean score $= 15.4$, $S.D. = 2.9$, $r = .61$; score is average per letter for five letters.) It indicates that if only girls who scored at least 14 had been hired, none of them would have been rated "below average" and many would have been rated "above average" or "superior." From Psychological Corporation *Test Service Bulletin*, No. 38, December 1949.

only those applicants who make scores of 14 or higher on the test, he can expect that all of them will succeed and none of them really fail. In a tight labor market, he may have to hire people who get scores lower than 12 in order to get enough workers to keep things going. In this case, though, he anticipates that there will be a larger number of failures, but still not as many as there would have been if he had not used the test. For the employment manager a test is mainly a tool to use in increasing the *number* of successes, and lessening the *number* of failures. He is not concerned about the meaning of individual scores and patterns of scores. He realizes that some errors in selection occur as the test is used—that some persons with high scores do not make good—but he does not worry about these failures as long as there are not too many of them. Another possible error does not bother him at all—that because of low test scores he may have turned down a few persons who might have been outstanding successes.

There are many other situations besides those pertaining to work and education where tests contribute to decisions about people. In clinics the basic question is: "Just what is *wrong* here?" When a mentally ill patient enters a hospital, the first step in treating him is to try to find out what he is suffering from. If his general symptoms suggest either schizophrenia or an organic psychosis arising from a brain disease, his psychologist uses tests which, previous research has shown, differentiate between schizophrenic and organic patients. Since such diagnostic decisions are typically made by teams of experts rather than by a psychologist alone, the clues obtained from testing are supplemented by clues coming from other types of examination. In this case, an analysis of the patient's electroencephalogram (a record of electrical activity in the brain) and a physician's report about the patient's illnesses that might have produced brain damage would almost certainly be brought in. Tests are also used in this diagnostic way by reading specialists who try to pin-point what a slow reader's trouble is so that they can teach him what he has not learned in the regular schoolroom, by speech therapists who suspect that personality characteristics are relevant in the case of a stutterer, and by many other clinical and educational workers.

Such clinical uses differ from the selection situations discussed above in that test results need only furnish clues or hypotheses, which are always checked against other kinds of information about the person being studied. Thus, it is even more true here than in selection situations that tests may be of some value even though they are not highly reliable or completely valid for the purpose for which the examiner is using them. His ingenuity in thinking of ways to track down new clues about his patient's difficulty is what counts. He may even improvise some testing procedures that have never been studied systematically at all. If such procedures furnish hypotheses he can check against facts drawn from the patient's behavior, symptoms, and history, they have served their purpose. But that some novel unstandardized procedure is a workable test in a particular case (or even in 10 or 100 cases) does not constitute evidence that it is a useful tool for decision-making in *all* comparable situations. In diagnostic testing many instruments are in fact resorted to that do not meet the standards we set up in Chapter 3. This charge applies to a large proportion of the projective tests in clinical use. Therefore, we must be

Applications
of Tests
and
Measurements

careful not to conclude that they would be valuable when decisions are made entirely or mainly on the basis of test results alone. It is imperative that hypotheses based on tests that are less than adequate be checked against other sources of information.

Decisions by People

When decisions are to be made *by* an individual, as when a person seeks counseling, the utilization of test information is more complicated. Even when a test has a fairly high validity coefficient, each test score has quite a range of criterion scores associated with it. This is illustrated in Table 6 on page 90—persons with scores in the 10–11 class ranged from Below Average to Above Average on the criterion variable.

In struggling with the problem of whether to take the job as an oil company geologist or return to Graduate School to work for a Ph.D., for example, Jerry may wish to compare his general intellectual ability with that of other graduate students by means of a test like the Graduate Record Examination. But how shall he use the information given him that his score is 450? If norm tables tell him that this is just a little below the average level for graduate students in geology, he cannot be certain of below-average grades. Tabulations of what students in the past have done show that some students with scores like his come out with straight A's, others with C minus averages. Which kind is he? Error in either direction in his decision will be costly to him. If he decides to go ahead with graduate work and finds after a year or two that he is not going to be able to qualify for a Ph.D., he will feel that he has wasted a considerable fraction of his life. Further, he may not at that time have as good a position offered him as the oil company is offering him now. If, on the other hand, he decides *against* graduate work on the basis of his below-average score, he may be cutting himself off for the rest of his life from the highest levels of his profession, levels that at least *some* persons with scores like his reach. If Jerry is to make a good decision here, he must consider many factors. His test score is only one.

Some Guiding Principles

Clearly, the standards we apply in selecting tests should be set according to the planned uses of test results. We can never say, "This is the *best* intelligence test. Go ahead and use it for everything," or "This is a *good* test of emotional maturity in children." We always ask, "*Who* is to use the results of this test, and for *what* purposes?" before we can say anything about its probable contribution to decision-making.

For all the classes of decision we have been considering, we can lay down some general guide lines about using tests. In selection situations, it is advisable to *try out* a proposed test without using the scores for selection purposes. After we find out how testees in this trial group turn out, we can set up an expectancy table like that in Table 6. This will show how many failures there were altogether and how many there would have been had a particular passing score been set in order to disqualify some applicants at the outset. We can then analyze the probable effects of different minimum scores before deciding what procedure to use in the future.

In making preliminary tryouts, it is advisable whenever possible to compare several tests. Often some combination of two or three turns out to be more effective than any one alone. Financial and practical considerations always enter into decisions, of course. It may be that the use of Test A will reduce the failure rate from 29 per cent to 10 per cent. But if the examination must be given to each applicant individually, it may make better sense to use instead a short group quiz, Test B, even if it only reduces the failure rate to 14 per cent. In dollars and cents the cost of the extra failures may be lower than the cost of the individual testing.

We must often weigh the expense of a testing program to eliminate unpromising candidates against the cost of training. If a job merely calls for a skill anyone can learn in a few days, the use of tests to select particularly apt persons is usually not worthwhile. On the other hand, if long training periods and costly equipment are needed to make a person skillful, even a highly expensive testing program to pick out the most promising candidates for training can be justified, as in the Air Force selection program discussed in Chapter 5.

In summary, a good rule when using tests to select people is: Get information about their *specific validity*—what they accomplish in a particular situation. A good rule in diagnostic situations is: Seek out as many different *kinds* of information as possible on the given problem. Use tests as one source of ideas about the case, but do not rest the final decision on test results alone. Corroborating evidence must support them.

Where a person wishes to use tests to help him make decisions about his own life, the most important principle is to choose tests very carefully. It is here that the standards set up in Chapter 3 are most essential. For a test to contribute substantially to vital decisions, it must be reliable enough so that an individual's score gives a fairly accurate indication of the person's relative standing in terms of the characteristic being measured. It must have a long enough history to make plain just what trait it is measuring. And we must know what *predictions* can reasonably be made from it of progress along specified lines for persons with low, medium, and high scores.

What we do not always recognize about tests as tools is that a test is not built all at once like a house or a machine. It *develops* over a period of years, and its usefulness *grows* as experience with it increases. We could range all the varieties of test we have considered along a scale that would show how well developed they are at present. A brand-new test, no matter how ingenious an idea it represents or how great the social need for it, would be at the bottom of such a "development" scale. A test like the Stanford-Binet, which has been in continuous use since 1916, would stand at the top, for a well-trained examiner familiar with the large body of knowledge that has grown up around it knows what it measures and what kinds of decisions it facilitates.

As we have seen, situations differ in the degree of development required in a test. For diagnostic work, well-developed tests are to be preferred whenever they are available, but even tests low on the scale can serve as sources of hypotheses if such hypotheses are carefully checked against nontest data. In selecting people for jobs, we also prefer to use well-developed tests, but we can bring in newer ones if we are in a position to run tryout studies. In counseling, well-developed tests are most essential, although even here a new test can sometimes prove a fruitful source of ideas for the person himself to check out against nontest evidence. In such a case, however, it is especially important for the counselor to know enough to make clear which kinds of test results cannot stand alone. Tests are tools, and their value depends chiefly on the skill of their users.

TESTS AS TOOLS IN RESEARCH
ON GROUP DIFFERENCES

From the earliest intelligence tests on, the principal purpose of such instruments has been to compare individuals in situations like those we have been discussing. But almost immediately another possible use became apparent— to facilitate research on age-old problems of *group differences*. For centuries before the era of psychological testing, people had been arguing about whether or not women were intellectually inferior to men, the dark races to the white races, and the peasant and artisan to the aristocrat. Men had built up complex social structures on assumptions of such group differences. Skeptical thinkers had again and again questioned these assumptions. Yet neither side had had any way to prove or disprove them. Perhaps, it was now hoped, the new psychological tests would be exactly the tools that had been needed all along. Perhaps at last these vexing questions could be settled.

Investigators tackling group differences have turned to intelligence tests more than any other variety. For one reason, general comparisons of intellectual capacity seem to fit most closely the old controversies—one question, for example, that during the nineteenth century seemed most urgent to many educators was whether female intellects were really equal to the strain of college education. For another reason, intelligence tests were available earlier than any of the others. Special-ability tests came later, personality tests later still.

The evaluation of the mass of evidence about group differences is a complex task. One source of ambiguity is the nature of tests as measuring instruments. Early workers did not see any problem here. It was only after tests reached a fairly high stage of development that researchers began to be concerned about it. One difficulty is the matter we took up in Chapter 1— that the numbers in which test scores are expressed do not constitute measurement scales in the sense that measurements of quantities like height and weight do. But before it was clear, first, that there are different *levels* of measurement, and second, that even though tests do not usually give us ratio scales, we can work legitimately with interval or ordinal scales, it looked to many honest researchers as though mental tests were simply unusable as instruments of science.

An even more serious difficulty is whether the *content* of tests makes them suitable for group comparisons. Now, all tests are made up of questions or tasks to be presented to subjects. As explained earlier, it became apparent soon after mental testing was invented that an individual's success with such tasks depended on a complex combination of inherited potential and experience. If our only concern is to find out where one *individual* stands, we can overcome this problem fairly well by choosing a test whose content is appropriate for his background and then comparing him with appropriate norm groups. But when we attempt to compare two groups, the question about whether the content and norms of the test are equally appropriate for both groups becomes serious. There is no altogether satisfactory way of answering it. As we saw in Chapter 3, any test score—MA, IQ, percentile rank, stanine, and so on—tells us where a person stands in relation to a particular reference group with regard to a particular tested characteristic. Even if we make our norm groups representative of the total population, we do not automatically render the questions fair to minorities within the population.

For a while, many psychologists assumed that verbal tests were most subject to criticism on these counts, and that if nonverbal, or nonlanguage, tests could be devised, group comparisons would be fair, regardless of subjects' cultural backgrounds. Experience has clearly indicated that this assumption is unsound—that children must *learn*, for example, to see details in pictures and to manipulate geometrical forms rapidly and accurately, just as they must learn to talk, to read, and to figure. Cultural groups that give their children little or no experience in looking at pictures or in putting odd-shaped blocks together cannot be considered inferior in innate ability if their young average lower scores than the usual norm groups, which have been made up of children who obtain such experience as a matter of course. It seems unlikely now that we will ever find a type of test question or task that can be considered really "culture-free," or as some prefer to call it, "culture-fair."

Must we then give up the aim of exploring group differences by means of mental tests? While there might be some variation among social scientists in their answers, the majority would probably say "No." What is called for is a *program of research* in each area of doubt. We ought first to find out what differences exist and then to carry out a long series of special studies designed to tell us what these differences mean. On the critical topics of sex, race, and social-class differences, such programs of research have occurred mainly by chance, and each new study has added something to what was previously known. In the paragraphs to follow, we shall try to make clear where we stand now on each of these three issues, recognizing that the research on which our knowledge rests has been somewhat haphazard and that the last word has not yet been said.

Sex Differences

Let us look first at what we know about differences between the sexes. The first general conclusion we can state is that carefully constructed intelligence tests do not produce

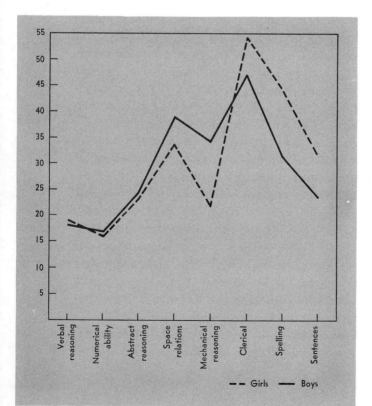

Figure 20. Average scores made by 6900 9th grade boys and 7400 9th grade girls on the Differential Aptitude Tests. (Bennett, G. K., Seashore, H. G., and Wesman, A. G. Manual for Differential Aptitude Tests, 3rd ed., p. 26. Psychological Corporation.)

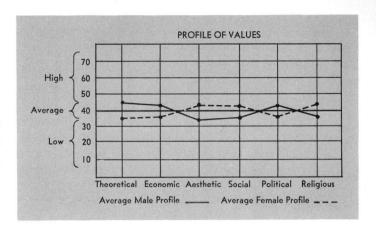

Figure 21. Sex differences on the Allport-Vernon-Lindzey Study of Values. (Allport, G. W., Vernon, P. E., and Lindzey, G. Study of values, 3rd ed. Boston: Houghton Mifflin, 1960.)

significant discrepancies in total score between males and females. There is, however, some divergence in the *pattern* of scores on special abilities. If a test is made up of several separate subtests, the profiles for the sexes characteristically differ even though the over-all score does not, as Figure 20 graphically shows. The nature of this difference in pattern suggests that it may arise from educational influences and from the characteristic expectations families have for boys and for girls. For the differences are in line with stereotypes about the sexes—that females are more verbal, for example, and males more mathematical.

Personality tests, too, have been used in many studies comparing men with women or boys with girls. The general conclusion we can draw from these studies is that the sexes differ more in personality traits than they do in abilities. For example, Figure 21 shows the kinds of results that have been obtained with an inventory measuring different kinds of values. Women get higher scores than men do on aesthetic, social, and religious values, but men score higher on theoretical, economic, and political values. And there are other instances: Work with vocational interest tests also leads to conclusions of sex differences. Evidence from personality questionnaires supports observations of behavior that males are considerably more aggressive than females. Females usually score higher than males on measures of neurotic tendency. And so on with many other kinds of personality traits.

Few research workers would at present question the existence of personality differences between the sexes. What they are more interested in now is their sources. At first questions about the origin of sex differences were usually formulated in some simple "either-or" manner—for example, "Are differences *biological* or *social?*" But we have come to realize that such statements are far too simple. Sex differences are both biological and social. Boy and girl babies begin life with differences in body structure and body chemistry, and their patterns of growth are dissimilar. Partly because of these

Applications
of Tests
and
Measurements

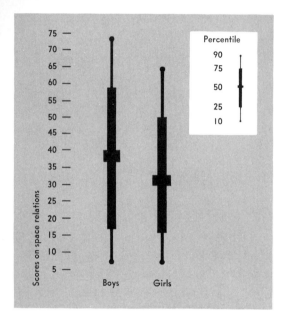

Figure 22. A comparison of the distributions of scores on the DAT Test of Space Relations for 9th grade boys and girls. (Bennett, G. K., Seashore, H. G., and Wesman, A. G. Manual for Differential Aptitude Tests, 3rd ed., p. 26. Psychological Corporation.)

facts, partly because of the complex training of their own sex roles, parents treat the two somewhat differently and expect different things of them. By the time children have reached nursery-school age, they have developed ideas of their own about what it means to be a boy or a girl. So we need to put all these factors together to explain what sex differences in average scores mean. A great deal of research is going on in this area, motivated in part by the thought that if we can understand the complex factors in this differential development, we may also get clues to understanding other complex aspects of personality. Questions like "How much and what kind of influence do fathers have as compared to mothers?" come to mind.

In thinking about sex differences, we must always keep in mind that most figures give us *averages,* and that within each sex there is a large amount of variation. Graphs of whole distributions of tests scores nearly always show a great deal of *overlapping.* If we look carefully at Figure 22, for example, we find that the *highest* girl in the group scores far above the average for boys, and the *lowest* boy scores far below the average for girls. What this tells us is that we can never use group averages in making decisions about individuals. That girls average much lower than boys on tests of mathematical reasoning is completely irrelevant when we must make a decision about whether one individual, Mary Eustis, should be admitted to an institute of technology. The question here is "What score did *Mary* make?" not "What is the average score for *girls?*"

Race Differences

In the United States comparisons of Negro and white groups have been made again and again. To the simple question "Do differences exist?" the answer is clearly "Yes." In study after study, in various parts of the United States and Canada, when standardized intelligence or achievement tests are given groups of Negroes and white school children or adults (as in the armed forces), the *average* for the white group is significantly higher than the *average* for the Negro group. (Individuals, of course, vary widely.)

If we are to go beyond this fact of differences in averages, however, we must look at other research investigations designed to throw light on what the differences mean. When the reports of Negro-white comparisons appeared in the 1920's, most psychologists were still assuming that intelligence tests measured pure innate ability, unaffected by experience or training. If this were indeed the case, then one could conclude without too much doubt what Americans and Europeans had been concluding for centuries without benefit of test evidence—that black men were intellectually inferior to white men. But as it became disturbingly apparent that intelligence test scores reflect environmental influences as well as innate potential, the easy conclusion about the biological origin of race differences became less tenable. Research workers began to search for "natural experiments"—special situations of some sort— that would enable them to rule out some hypotheses about the meaning of the findings and to support others.

One of these hypotheses was that Negroes do less well than whites because the most common tests are unfair to them. If this were the main reason for the differences, we might expect to find certain tests in which Negroes equal or exceed the white averages. This particular hypothesis has not stood up very well under investigation. Although particular studies often show that Negroes are more handicapped on some kinds of test item than on others, on no type of question or task that is useful in measuring intelligence do Negroes, as a group, excel. The difference in average scores does not seem to be a mere matter of verbal or spatial ability, or speed of response.

A more productive line of investigation opened up when it was noted that the averages on the Army Alpha test used in World War I were actually higher for Negroes in some northern states than they were for whites in some southern states. For example, the average for white recruits from Arkansas, Kentucky, and Mississippi was about 41. Negroes from New York averaged 44, Negroes from Ohio 49, Negroes from Illinois 47. Two possible explanations for these findings occurred to those who studied them—one, that superior Negroes tended to migrate to Northern cities, the other, that educational advantages in the North led to better performance on intelligence tests.

So special studies were set up to investigate these hypotheses. These studies have fostered the conclusion that it is the educational factor that is really crucial. Research by Otto Klineberg in New York and by E. S. Lee in Philadelphia showed clearly that among Negroes in Northern schools those who had attended for long stretches scored higher than those who had been going for shorter periods.

There is some evidence, however, that differences in the amount and quality of *formal* schooling do not account for all the obtained Negro-white differences. H. A. Tanser in a study of a Canadian town where Negro and white children had attended the same schools since Civil War days reported higher averages for white children in spite of the apparent equality in educational opportunity. There are probably other and more complex factors than legal equality that determine how well children can take advantage of the educational opportunities they have. For one thing, a good deal of education occurs before children enter public school. In very poor homes where there are no books, no pictures, and few toys, and where little special attention is given to stimulating children's mental growth, the "aptitude for education" we measure by means of intelligence tests probably does not develop satisfactorily. Because the socio-economic level of Negro families is lower than that of white families in most communities, such a handicap for Negro children might well occur. Lee's study in Philadelphia showed that the highest-scoring group of Negro children was composed of Philadelphia-born children who had attended kindergarten. And these children consistently scored about three IQ points higher than the Philadelphia-born group who had *not* gone to kindergarten. Perhaps the kindergarten experience provides preschool education often lacking in poor children's homes.

Here again it is important to remember that there is a great deal of variation in intelligence within the Negro groups, just as there is within the white group. Averages never tell the whole story. It is not at all uncommon for individual Negro students to make extremely high scores on intelligence tests and to stand at the top of their classes. In all the group comparisons we have mentioned, in the distributions of scores a substantial minority of the Negro scores fall above the mean for whites, and a considerable number of the white scores fall below the mean for Negroes. To evaluate an individual we must test him individually.

Because research on race differences in intelligence has been going on for so many years and has been approached from so many angles, it is possible to find somewhere in the mass of accumulated data support for almost any argument. The segregationist can use the well-documented differences in average score as evidence that placing all the Negro children of a community into white schools may lead to an appreciable decrease in the educational level of the schools. The integrationist can point to the impressive figures which show that attendance in good schools produces increases in scores on intelligence and achievement tests as evidence that wiping out the educational handicaps now burdening many Negro children is of the highest importance. We must be very cautious about accepting any simple conclusions based on "scientific" studies of race differences in the United States. In order to evaluate what we hear we must be somewhat familiar with the whole body of research in this area rather than just isolated pieces of it.

Decisions about social policy are ultimately grounded on many considerations, not the least of which are ideals of justice and equality. Research results, whatever they are, do not *determine* such decisions. Their main value for policy-makers, however, lies in helping them *predict* what the probable consequences of various alternative programs will be. Studies of Negro-white differences on measurable traits can serve this purpose.

Social-Class Differences

Another research topic that has received special attention since the early days of mental testing is the problem of relationship of social class to intelligence. Here, too, it is easy to find group differences, but not so easy to determine what they mean. Doing so has required a long sequence of related studies.

One thread runs through them all: When we sort people out according to their social status in the community and give them intelligence or achievement tests, we find fairly large differences between the averages of the different groups. In both world wars, comparisons of men with different occupations were clear on this point. On the General Classification Test used in World War II,·for example, accountants and lawyers averaged about 128, clerical workers about 118, electricians and other skilled craftsmen about 109, miners and farmhands about 91. When the children of men from different occupations are tested in school, they show the same differences as their fathers. Terman and Merrill, for example, found, in the carefully selected sample of the population on which Stanford-Binet norms are based, the following average IQ's for two- to five-and-a-half-year-old children from families at different occupational levels:

Professional	115
Semi-professional and managerial	112
Clerical, skilled trades, retail business	108
Semi-skilled, minor clerical and business	104
Rural owners	98
Slightly skilled	97
Day labor, urban and rural	94

And they discovered similar differences for other age levels. Further, studies in which the social-class rating is based on community regard as well as on occupation alone yield the same intelligence differentiation between children from middle- and upper-class families and children from lower-class families. Finally, farm children typically average lower than city children.

The subsequent investigations of the meaning of these differences have principally revolved around two hypothetical pivots. The first is that intelligence tests, constructed as they usually are by middle-class psychologists and educators, are unfair to lower-class children and thus constantly produce underestimates of their intellectual potentialities. According to this line of thinking, what we need most are tests made up of problems and questions more representative of the attitudes and thought processes of lower-class children. A large-scale research project at the University of Chicago directed by Kenneth Eells analyzed the responses children from different social classes made to test questions. Eells and Allison Davis then constructed a new test they called the Davis-Eells Games, which was made up exclusively of the types of problems on which the classes differed least. As Figure 23 shows, the test

Figure 23. Sample items from the Davis-Eells Games Primary A, *by Allison Davis and Kenneth Eells. (New York: Harcourt, Brace & World, Copyright 1952. Reproduced by permission.)*

is made up of pictures of real-life situations and practical, common-sense questions about them. Unfortunately for the hypothesis on which it is based, in tryouts of the test in a number of communities, lower-class children still average lower than middle- and upper-class children, as on the more conventional intelligence tests. Furthermore, scores on the Davis-Eells Games do not predict success in school work as well as other intelligence scores do, so its practical contribution to educational decisions is limited. This whole line of research has made the hypothesis that social-class differences arise primarily from the type of test used look less promising than it once did.

Arguments about whether social-class differences in intelligence and school achievement arise from hereditary or environmental sources are less common than they once were. Our awareness that the intellectual development of any individual under any circumstances involves a complex combination of the two factors has settled this controversy along with many others. What now challenges educational researchers is the quest for ways of making the school environment more stimulating to lower-class children than it typically is.

We need to know, too, why the children of some lower-class families move up the social ladder to become much more successful than their parents were. And we need to know why some drop out of school at the earliest possible time, apparently immune to formal education. Studies of creativity, of achievement motivation, and of many other complex attitudes and motives are all relevant to these problems.

In this field too, we must always keep in mind the fact of overlapping between the social classes. It is not just a Horatio Alger myth that some poor boys become presidents—of corporations, of universities, or of the United States. That there is a wide range of talent within each social group is particularly important because of the vast difference between the classes in absolute size. That is, there are far more poor families than rich ones, far more skilled workers than professional men. In a careful study of a midwestern community, Robert J. Havighurst and L. L. Janke (1944) identified the following class structure:

Class A. Wealthy families (2 per cent of the population)
Class B. Professional men, officials, and leading businessmen (6 per cent of the population)
Class C. Small businessmen, lesser professional workers, some skilled workers, white-collar workers (37 per cent of the population)
Class D. Semi-skilled workers and laborers, hardworking and respectable people (43 per cent of the population)
Class E. Lowest occupational groups with poor reputation in the community (12 per cent of the population)

Even if it were true that half the children from Classes A and B and only one-tenth of the children from Groups D and E were bright enough to qualify for the best colleges and the most demanding positions, there would still be a larger absolute number of D and E children in the select group than of A and B children. For half of 8 per cent yields four persons out of every hundred, and one-tenth of 55 per cent yields five. As the need for trained intelligence in all parts of our society has become more urgent, the whole distribution of intelligence ratings in each social class has come to seem more important than the average rating for the group. We cannot run our complex civilization without developing the talents of individuals from the groups with the lower averages.

AGE DIFFERENCES IN ADULTS

In explaining how intelligence tests for children are constructed, we discussed at some length the importance of age differences, and the characteristics of mental-growth curves. The question of age differences in adults is less urgent, but over the years it has received some consideration.

It was assumed to start with that elderly adults would do less well than young adults on intelligence tests, as they do on physical examinations and strength tests. Most of the research done in the 20's and the 30's led to the same conclusions. W. R. Miles and C. C. Miles, for example, reported that although the average IQ for 20-year-olds with an eighth grade education was 100, the average for 50-year-olds with the same amount of schooling was 90, and the average for 80-year-olds only about 75. Similar differences were found in age groups with more education. Twenty-year-olds with college training averaged about 120; 50-year-olds about 110. The facts that persons in the older groups had grown up in very different circumstances, had not become "test-wise" as children, and had perhaps not answered examination questions for years were ignored when the results were discussed.

But as in the studies of sex, race, and social class, research on the meaning and origin of these age differences gradually accumulated. Some investigators analyzed the results with different kinds of test materials and different kinds of testing conditions, and found that on all performance tests older subjects ranked lower than on verbal tests; similarly, on speed tests they rated lower than on power tests. On the other hand, in several studies older testees actually averaged higher than younger ones on the vocabulary tests that constitute an important part of many general intelligence measures.

In the 1950's the results of several longitudinal projects were reported—studies in which the same adults were tested at different periods of their lives. In the most elaborate of these William A. Owens located 127 men who had taken Army Alpha at the time they entered college right after the end of World War I and retested them with the same test 30 years later, when they were in their late 40's. Instead of scoring lower than they originally did, these men averaged higher on the test as a whole and on most of its subtests.

What such studies show is that there need not be an inevitable decline in mental powers from youth at least through middle age. Educational influences operate here, as in the other group comparisons we have considered. The men in the study referred to above were for the most part college graduates who probably continued to educate themselves by reading, thinking, and conversing after their college years were over. They lived in a period during which there was a constant increase in the amount of educational stimulation available in most parts of the United States—books and libraries, correspondence and extension courses, radio and television programs. It seems probable now that in earlier studies one reason persons over 50 scored so much lower than younger adults was that they had grown up and spent most of their lives in a much less rich educational environment.

Older and younger adults have been compared on tests of special abilities and personality as well as intelligence. On the average, scores for groups of persons who are at or beyond middle age usually turn out to be poorer than those for younger groups if the test requires speed of response, perception of details, or the solution of novel or unfamiliar problems. Even in these special areas, however, adults of all ages seem to be able to maintain skills they acquired early in life. Thus, they have less of an occupational handicap than they are often thought to have. In personality characteristics and interests, the differences between adults of all ages are small, except for the very old who show more personality difficulties of various kinds—anxiety, social isolation, neurotic and psychotic trends. These, however, may well be outgrowths of the strains and difficult circumstances that come with retirement, bereavement, and ill health rather than inevitable psychological handicaps concomitant with aging.

Within any age group there is, once again, wide variation from person to person in all characteristics for which we have tests. We simply cannot judge how intelligent, how skillful, or how well adjusted a person is by considering age alone. All retirement plans run into this difficulty. Many individual 65-year-olds are well above the mean for 25-year-olds even in speed and flexibility, in which youth as a rule clearly excels age. Again we must emphasize the same conclusions stated for sex and race differences: Differences *within* a group are larger than differences *between* groups. The assessment of an individual must be an individual matter.

THE RELATIONSHIP BETWEEN MENTAL AND PHYSICAL TRAITS

When measurements of psychological characteristics became available, it was natural that men should have used them in the search for answers to some questions that had intrigued thinking persons for years—questions about the relationship of physical and mental qualities. Diverse theories and various bits of "folk wisdom" needed to be tested. Is a sound mind most likely to develop in a sound body? Does too rapid intellectual growth stunt bodily development? Do persons of different build tend to differ also in temperament, as has been assumed since centuries before Shakespeare had Caesar say of Cassius:

Let me have men about me that are fat,
Sleek-headed men, and such as sleep o' nights:
Yon Cassius has a lean and hungry look;
He thinks too much. Such men are dangerous.

From a large amount of research on such problems, the most general conclusion we can draw is that the relationships between measured physical and mental traits are too slim to be of practical value in judging people. There *is*, it seems, a slight tendency for desirable traits to go together. High intelligence, for example, is a little more likely to appear in the larger and stronger children than in the smaller and weaker ones. But the obtained correlations in studies on this matter are seldom higher than .20. And there are so many exceptions to the general trend that any combination of mental and physical abilities can occur. Some Phi Beta Kappas are healthy; others are sickly. Some athletes are brilliant; others are not. Some studious girls are beautiful; others are plain.

Evidence points to a somewhat closer relationship between body build and temperament—that is, emotional and motivational characteristics rather than abilities. The classification of body builds most widely used at present is the one worked out by William H. Sheldon. In this system, *endomorphy* is the predominance of soft roundness in body structures, *mesomorphy* the predominance of muscle and bone, and *ectomorphy* the predominance of thinness and fragility. Sheldon's research seems to demonstrate that the more endomorphic a person is, the more he is relaxed, friendly, and pleasure-loving in his behavior and relationships with other people. Mesomorphy is related to vigor and adventurousness, ectomorphy to intellectual and introverted traits. When we consider all the available evidence along with Sheldon's, however, we are forced to conclude that such relationships between physique and temperament are not very close. In some studies the correlations obtained seem mainly to reflect the inclination of persons taking part in the research, especially those doing the rating, to expect certain relationships and so unconsciously to slant their data to produce them. On the whole, we can say, as we did after discussing group comparisons, that if we really wish to know how intelligent, adventurous, athletic, or friendly an individual is, the soundest way to find out is to evaluate that trait directly. We cannot judge a person by appearance much more accurately than we can by sex, race, or age.

HEREDITY AND ENVIRONMENT

The most persistent question throughout all the years of psychological testing is whether the differences revealed among individuals arise from hereditary or environmental sources. We have touched on this question in several previous sections, emphasizing again and again the point that the traits measured by intelligence, aptitude, achievement, and personality tests are *not* pure native characteristics, and that they are based on the experience individuals have had as well as on their native potentialities. It is essential, though, to realize that this does not mean that heredity has nothing to do with these traits. That we cannot *measure* pure native capacity, uncontaminated by environmental influences, does not prove that there is no such thing or that at birth all individuals are alike.

Pragmatically this presents no problem. For in making decisions and plans about human beings, we do not usually need to know whether their strengths and weaknesses rest mainly on hereditary or environmental foundations. We can make allowances for a poor boy from a backwoods town whose schooling has been meager and who has had almost no access to books and ideas and so scores only at the tenth percentile on a college aptitude test. But the fact remains that he is likely to have a difficult time in college competition and that it is almost impossible for him to wipe out the effects of 18 years of intellectual starvation by giving himself an enriched diet during his four college years. Attributing his educational inadequacies to his previous environment does not make them any easier to change. On the other hand, characteristics known to be based on hereditary causes often can be changed. Just as a person with diabetes can use insulin to keep symptoms from appearing, so a child with what appears to be hereditary tendencies toward emotional instability can be trained in habits that will keep the instability from handicapping him in the business of living. He can learn, for example, to clench his fists and count ten instead of throwing a temper tantrum, to stay out of social situations that irritate him, to choose an occupation where he can work at his own pace. How susceptible a trait is to modification through learning does not usually depend on the extent to which it arises from either nature or nurture.

What present-day students of the problem hope to accomplish is to pin down the interactions of specific hereditary tendencies in individuals with specific environmental influences. It does not seem altogether impossible that we may some day know enough about this interaction to supply for each person, as he develops, the special environment in which his particular personality is most likely to fluorish. Instead of thinking about *good* stock and *good* environments, we need to have in mind *different* hereditary potentialities, capable of making diverse contributions to our common life given the appropriate conditions. To go back to the medical example of the last paragraph, what a diabetic needs in order to remain healthy is not just a general "good" diet, but one especially tailored for his condition. Other human characteristics about which we do not as yet know so much probably follow the same principle.

Psychologists have made only a beginning on this large undertaking. So far the research on heredity and human behavior has been largely concerned with general intelligence. Even after it became apparent that individual differences in test score were related to differences in the educational backgrounds of the testees, investigators still hoped to be able to arrive at some figure that would express what the relative *weights* of hereditary and environmental determiners were. They thought for a time that it would be possible to make statements like this: "Intelligence is determined 80 per cent by heredity, 20 per cent by environment." Most of the persons who have worked on this problem have now given up this aim. The trouble is that *adding* up components does not produce a person. It is the interaction that is important —the continuous transformation of a complex pattern in which hereditary and environmental elements are no longer distinguishable. But even though this research on the hereditary basis of intelligence did not achieve its purpose, it produced a body of information and a set of research tools that are useful in our study of a variety of questions relating to heredity.

The most significant findings have come out of studies of *twins*. Identical, or *monozygotic,* twins are ideal subjects for research on heredity, because they have identical sets of genes. In such cases, the two individuals have grown from a single fertilized egg cell that separated into parts at the time of the first cell division. Thus, any differences in behavior, ability, or personality between such twins must be based on some environmental influence. It cannot be hereditary.

In twin studies, two research designs are most commonly used. The first is to compare the amount of resemblance in identical twin pairs with the amount of resemblance in other pairs of children. The first step is to find out how much alike the identical twin pairs are, on the average, in some characteristic, such as intelligence. The next step is to see how much alike fraternal, or *dizygotic,* twins are (those growing out of two fertilized egg cells, and thus no more alike in their gene pattern than any two siblings are). Often a third step is added—to see how much alike non twin siblings are. Because resem-

Figure 24. Correlations between pairs of children in the same family for height and for intelligence. (Twin correlations from Woodworth, R. S. Heredity and environment. New York Soc. Sci. Res. Council, 1941. Sibling correlations from Conrad, H. S. and Jones, H. E. in Yearbk. Nat. Soc. Stud. Educ., 1940, 39, II, 97–141; and Pearson, K. and Lee, A. Biometriks, 1903, 2, 357–462.)

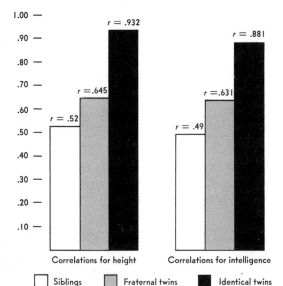

r = .932

r = .881

r = .645

r = .631

r = .52

r = .49

Correlations for height

Correlations for intelligence

☐ Siblings   ▨ Fraternal twins   ■ Identical twins

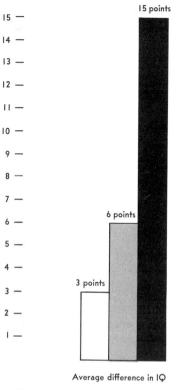

Average difference in IQ

☐ Identical twins reared together

▨ Identical twins reared apart

■ Unrelated children

Figure 25. Average IQ differences for pairs of children with different degrees of relationship (Woodworth, R. S. Heredity and environment. *New York: Soc. Sci. Res. Council, 1941.)*

blances between children in the same family can arise from either heredity or environment, or from both, the comparisons of different kinds of sibling pairs enable us to sort out some of these determiners and draw some tentative conclusions about whether or not any particular trait has a hereditary basis. If it has, we would expect identical twins to resemble each other most closely because both heredity and environment are likely to affect them in similar ways. Siblings of different ages would be the least similar, since some of the family environmental influences on their development would be dissimilar because of the time lapse between one child and the other. Fraternal twins should be somewhere in between, since they are no more alike in heredity than ordinary siblings are, but they do experience the family environment at the same time. For intelligence, this is, in fact, exactly what we find, as shown in Figure 24. Since this pattern of correlations is highly similar to that for height and other physical characteristics known to be determined principally by heredity, it seems reasonable to conclude that differences in intelligence also are based on heredity. A similar pattern has been found for some of the special abilities, such as mechanical and motor skills, and for some personality deviations, such as schizophrenia.

The second design in twin research involves comparing the resemblance between identical twins reared together with the resemblance between identical twins reared apart. Figure 25 illustrates what has been found. If heredity were *all*-important in determining an individual's intelligence or other psychological characteristics, it would be irrelevant whether identical twins were brought up in the same home and community or not. If environment were *all*-important, identical twins reared apart would be no more alike than random pairs of children. The principal reason we now know that neither of these extreme statements is true in the case of intelligence and a number of other mental characteristics is that research points to a reality somewhere between the two extremes. As Figure 25 shows, the average difference between twins *is* greater for those reared apart than for those reared together, but it is nowhere nearly as great as the difference between unrelated children.

It is these studies of identical twins reared in different homes and communities that have told us most about what *aspect* of the environment has the greatest effect on intelligence. In a thorough case study of 19 pairs of separated identical twins, H. H. Newman rated the environments separately for the educational and social advantages they provided. In all instances where one twin turned out to be much brighter than another, educational influences differed markedly. But social advantages did not seem to have much effect.

Other questions about the relative hereditary or environmental determination of various psychological characteristics have been approached in several other ways—studies of family histories, research on children in foster homes, animal-breeding studies. All these lines of investigation point to the general conclusion that many or most abilities and personality traits have some hereditary basis, but that their development is also affected by environmental influences. What we need now is research leading to more specific conclusions: What *sort* of effect do certain *kinds* of environment have on particular hereditary tendencies? We have passed the stage of argument over heredity versus environment, but we still have a great deal to survey and map in the area such arguments used to cover.

APPLICATIONS OF TESTS AND MEASUREMENTS— A FINAL WORD

The quantification of human traits, the invention of statistical methods appropriate for the kinds of numbers obtained, the construction of tests to measure abilities and personality characteristics—all these tasks have called for ingenuity, clear thinking, and a dash of cautious skepticism. The same qualities are needed by those who would use tests and measurements profitably. They are human tools designed for human purposes. By themselves they settle no theoretical arguments, treat no patients, educate no children, solve no social problems. But in the hands of skilled workers who understand them they can help us in all these undertakings. Each individual man or woman is required to make decisions about many matters as he carries on his work and associates with other people. It is the contribution tests and measurements make to the thinking on which such decisions are based that justifies their existence.

Selected Readings

Buros, E. K. Jr. (Ed.) *Mental measurements yearbook.* Highland Park, N. J.: Gryphon Press.

> There have been five editions of this indispensable reference book in the years from 1941 to 1959. In each of them, essential information about each particular test is summarized, and two or more reviewers comment on its strengths and weaknesses.

Cronbach, Lee J. *Essentials of psychological testing* (2nd ed.). New York: Harper, 1960.

> This is one of the best complete surveys of the whole field of psychological testing. More information about any of the tests mentioned in the present book is obtainable there, and a great many other tests are discussed in some detail.

Guilford, J. P. *Personality.* New York: McGraw-Hill, 1959.

> It is not likely that a student will wish to read this long and detailed book all at once, but he may wish to turn to particular chapters to find out what factor analysis has suggested about the basic dimensions or traits in a particular area, such as intelligence, temperament, or interests.

Hammond, Kenneth R., and Householder, James E. *Introduction to the statistical method.* New York: Knopf, 1962.

> In this book a psychologist and mathematician have combined their efforts to present the basic ideas of statistics in an exceptionally lucid and interesting way.

Hunt, J. McV. *Intelligence and experience.* New York: Ronald, 1961.

> This is the best synthesis to date of a large amount of research designed to show what intelligence is and how it grows.

Peterson, Joseph. *Early conceptions and tests of intelligence.* Yonkers: World Book, 1925.

> The early history of intelligence testing is covered here in much more detail than in other texts. It is often interesting for the stu-

dent to understand the thinking of the people who began the work in a major area.

Layton, W. L. *Counseling use of the Strong Vocational Interest Blank.* University of Minnesota Studies in Student Personnel Work, No. 8, 1958.

This short book gives the reader a good working knowledge of what the scores on the test mean without going into detail about technical matters.

Tyler, Leona E. *The psychology of human differences.* New York: Appleton-Century-Crofts, 1956.

In this more extensive book, many of the ideas discussed briefly in the present volume are gone into in more detail, with research evidence.

Woodworth, R. S. *Heredity and environment.* New York: Social Science Research Council Bulletin 47, 1941.

In this very clearly written monograph, Woodworth brought together the principal kinds of research evidence that had accumulated in connection with the heredity-environment controversy. The kind of synthesis he produced led to sounder conclusions about the origins of human abilities.

Index